CW00683943

BEC'S
Everyday
BITES

Over 80 recipes, all **under 500 calories**!

7 days of dinners to inspire a healthier lifestyle

Contents

Recipes

Bec's Everyday Bites

©2024 Rebecca Finley &
Meze Publishing Limited
First edition printed in 2024 in the UK
ISBN: 978-1-915538-19-2
Written by: Rebecca Finley
Edited by: Katie Fisher
Photography by: Timm Cleasby
Designed by: Phil Turner, Marc Barker
& Paul Cocker
PR: Emma Toogood & Lizzy Capps
Printed in UK by Bell and Bain Ltd, Glasgow

Published by Meze Publishing Limited
Unit 1b, 2 Kelham Square
Kelham Riverside
Sheffield S3 8SD
Web: www.mezepublishing.co.uk
Telephone: 0114 275 7709
Email: info@mezepublishing.co.uk

No part of this book shall be reproduced or transmitted in any form or by any means, electronic or mechanical, including photocopying, recording, or by any information retrieval system without written permission of the publisher.
Although every precaution has been taken in the preparation of this work, the publisher and author assume no responsibility for errors or omissions. Neither is any liability assumed for damages resulting from the use of this information contained herein.

Introduction

Hi! I'm Rebecca, and I've spent the past few years developing healthier recipes to help myself (and now to help you) make those small changes that make a big difference.

Bec's Bites started on social media about five years ago, when I decided to change my lifestyle and cook healthier meals for myself. However, when looking up many healthier recipes online, I found that they lacked flavour and seemed quite repetitive, even boring. As someone who has always enjoyed food and loved to cook, I thought it would be fun to share a few recipes that I had made at home because if I was struggling to find great recipes, surely other people were too.

Sure enough, the more recipes I shared, the more people joined the growing community on social media, and some were even beginning to cook my recipes and share the results with me as well as their friends and family! It always brings me so much joy to see people enjoying the recipes I create, and it's been a pleasure and a privilege to be able to help people cook healthier meals at home.

I'm so happy and grateful that I can now share some of my favourite recipes with you all in one place, instead of having to scroll through social media to find the recipe you're looking for. If you've followed my journey for a while, thank you so much for being here, and if you've just stumbled on this book, welcome! I hope you find many recipes here that you'll love and use for years to come.

Something that I and many others have struggled with when it comes to healthy eating is sticking to it. Not because I don't enjoy it, but because it can be more difficult than convenience foods and feels like a chore when you're really busy. Meal planning and prepping have helped me immensely, but I didn't always find them easy to do, and I know they are also both understood to be time consuming and a bit boring. This book is designed to help with all of that!

My recipes are separated into days of the week, from Monday to Sunday. Each chapter tackles a different challenge when it comes to healthy eating and takes into account the everyday struggles we all face throughout the week. For example, on Tuesdays and Wednesdays when you're in the thick of it and you want quicker, easier meals, One Pot Tuesdays focuses on meals made in one pan and traybakes, while Whip It Up Wednesdays focuses on recipes with minimal ingredients and short cooking times. As we all know, it can be easy to eat well during the week but then overindulge at the weekend, so my Fakeaway Fridays and Social Saturdays will help you to enjoy a well-deserved treat while still prioritising your health.

You'll notice some common themes throughout these recipes; they're all under 500 calories, with a focus on higher protein and fibre but less fat, and many include one of my favourite things – hidden veg – which are perfect for fussy family members. The main theme is simple though: delicious recipes that you can easily and comfortably cook at home. So, whether you're looking to change your lifestyle or just need some good old home-cooked recipe inspiration, this is the book for you.

Thank you for reading, and happy cooking!

Bec x

If you enjoy these recipes, please share them with me on social media – I'd love to see them!

Meal Planning

Meal planning is something I've done for many years now and it's changed the way I cook and eat. This book is designed to help you to plan your meals and whether you're a seasoned professional or just dipping your toes into the idea, there's something here for everyone.

There are so many benefits to meal planning, not least reducing waste and saving money by using up what you already have. There are many tips throughout the book that will help you find substitutes for ingredients, so don't let one pesky missing ingredient stop you from making a recipe you love!

Speaking of swapping ingredients, meal planning also helps you to be more creative with your food. It makes you think about what you can do with what you already have, and sometimes you end up creating or trying something you never would have thought of otherwise!

You'll likely find shopping easier and cheaper this way, as you'll be able to write a much more concise list and stay on track when it comes to actually doing the shopping, as you'll know you're getting exactly what you need. Bonus points if you can plan multiple meals (all with different tastes and textures) using similar ingredients!

Another benefit of meal planning is that it takes away decision fatigue, avoiding that question we all dread towards the end of each day: 'what shall I make for dinner?'. When you're busy, and your brain is juggling a million thoughts, it's so helpful to plan ahead. Even if you don't physically prepare anything in advance, mentally preparing takes at least one thing off your plate and honestly helps so much! You can plan around any commitments you have and know that you will be nourishing your body with a home-cooked meal, no matter how busy you are.

Finally, meal planning is the first step to meal prepping... but more on that later. For now, here's a few tips to help you plan your meals effectively.

1. Make time for yourself

First, make sure you set aside some time each week to plan your meals – I find it can be quite therapeutic! Taking some time for yourself helps you to gather your thoughts on the week ahead and allows you to go into it feeling organised (in one area of your life at least!). Make meal planning time non-negotiable and an enjoyable experience, rather than a chore – I like to sit down with my nice stationery, a cup of tea, and something good on TV in the background! It doesn't have to take ages either; I find half an hour or so is usually enough.

2. Check your supplies

The number one thing to do next is have a quick look at what's left in your fridge and cupboards, particularly perishable items that need to be used up like fruits, veggies, meats, fish, eggs, and open jars such as pesto or chutneys. Try to base meals around these ingredients where possible (check out the Throw It In Thursdays chapter for some new ideas on how to use up old ingredients!).

3. Check your calendar

For the week ahead, on days you know will be tiring, plan in something that takes minimal time and effort, and maybe uses fewer ingredients (the One Pot Tuesdays and Whip It Up Wednesdays chapters will be useful here). On days where you have a lot of commitments in the evenings, something you can prep in advance, already have made in the freezer, or leave in a slow cooker will mean that you don't have to spend hours cooking when you get home – check out the Meal Prep Mondays or Saucy Sundays chapter for ideas.

4. Get excited!

Make sure to plan in things that you're looking forward to! I have lived by having a 'Fakeaway Friday' each week for a long time now; it's something to get excited about, not too challenging to cook, and leaves you feeling content and refreshed for the weekend ahead. You can even make healthier home cooked meals on a Saturday, whether you're doing date night, dinner parties, family nights, or just a cosy night in on your own. Cooking something delicious and nutritious when you have the luxury of time can be so rewarding.

5. Old and new

I always try to plan in tried and tested old favourites as well as new dishes. Too many new recipes can leave you feeling overwhelmed, but too many old favourites can sometimes mean you get bored and we don't want either of those things! My rule of thumb is usually to try two or three new recipes each week, but you can go with whatever number you feel most comfortable with.

6. Variety is key

Make sure to plan enough variety in your week, whether that's through ingredients, cuisines, or cooking methods. Although we may end up buying a lot of similar ingredients each week – because we're familiar with them, or they suit our budgets better – with a handful of kitchen staples, it becomes much easier to enjoy something different each night!

7. Themes and goals

Use themes and goals to help you plan. I like to incorporate seasonal ingredients where possible (this can help keep costs down too) or think of a goal for the week, such as 'I want to eat seven portions of fruit and veg each day' or 'I want to eat fish twice this week'. Having these in your mind as you plan gives you something to focus on.

8. Listen to your body

If I'm craving something, like a burger, I write it down at the time and then make sure I add that food to my meal plan as soon as possible for the following week! As a woman, I personally find that my body needs different things throughout the month too; sometimes I need more comforting dishes and sometimes I need food that will energise me, such as particularly high protein and fibre foods. This works for planning family meals too; if anyone has a particularly high activity day coming up, you can cater to that with food.

9. Write it down

As you go through the week, if you see recipes online, in magazines, or even get recommendations from friends and family, write them down somewhere. Having a general list to look at before you even begin can really help to shape your meal plan and reduce the effort required. While we're on the topic of writing things down, don't forget to write down your meal plan! Whether that's on a specially made meal planning sheet, a chalkboard in the kitchen, or just in a note on your phone, it really helps to have a visual reference somewhere throughout the week. This also helps you to move things around if the week doesn't go exactly as planned.

10. Relax!

Sometimes, things just don't go to plan. Try to avoid beating yourself up when this happens. Hopefully, you'll find lots of recipes in this book that will help you to build up a stash of easy-to-reheat meals in your freezer for those days when things don't work out as you wanted. However, at the end of a long day, sometimes a freezer meal just isn't going to cut it! Take a break from cooking, enjoy the break from routine, and get back to it tomorrow.

Meal Prepping

Meal prepping can really help you to stay organised and make sure you're giving yourself the home-cooked meals you deserve, even when you're busy. But it gets a bad rap: many people think it's time consuming, or you have to do too much in advance, and some people think it's just boring!

I have to say, I thought all those things before I started making meal prepping work for me. If you're someone who enjoys spending your free time prepping ingredients, go for it! Many of the meals in this book will lend themselves to that, and I hope you find them helpful. For me, I like to fit meal prepping into the time I'm already in the kitchen, so it doesn't feel like an extra chore. I'm also someone who gets bored easily, so I struggle to eat the same meal on repeat for three or four days. To combat these things, here are a few things I do in my kitchen at home:

1. As mentioned, I like to maximise efficiency when I'm already in the kitchen. This might mean making two to four extra portions of a dish and then freezing the leftovers. If I'm already making a curry to serve two, for example, why not double it to serve four? It barely adds anything onto your prep and cooking times, and means you have extra food for lunches, or those days when you just can't be bothered to cook!

2. Similarly, when I'm already in the kitchen, I prepare other bits for the week ahead. This is where your meal plan will come in handy! For example, if I'm making mash on Monday and chips on Tuesday, I might peel and chop all the potatoes I need, then keep the chips in a pot of cold water until I need them on Tuesday. If I'm making meals that go with salad on Wednesday and Friday, I'll make up extra salad on the Wednesday and only dress half of it, saving the rest for Friday and saving me a job!

3. When it comes to leftovers and batch cooking, I really do HATE having the same thing again and again! I'm just not excited about my food then, and it can lead to me wanting to buy takeaways and convenience foods. What I do instead is repurpose my leftovers in interesting ways. You'll find lots of serving suggestions for many of the recipes in this book, so you should be able to do the same! For example, sauces and slow cooked meats can be served with chips, rice, veggies, or pasta and you can always bulk out a smaller portion with some extra vegetables. When I make a curry, I'll have it with rice the first time (and maybe some naan!) and then later use the remaining curry sauce on top of pizzas (like my naan pizzas in the Fakeaway Fridays chapter) and even add some to a toastie for lunch. There are so many amazing ways you can use up leftovers and it doesn't have to be repetitive.

4. When I prep extra food, nine times out of ten it's going in the freezer, rather than the fridge. If you follow the structure of this book, and always make something for 'meal prep' on a Monday, by the end of the month you'll have a whole week of dinners in the freezer. It's like having your own ready meals at home – and let's be honest, they're going to taste so much better when you make them yourself!

5. Finally, don't be afraid of convenience foods. Tinned, frozen and pre-chopped veg are all great ways to ensure you can maximise your efficiency when in the kitchen, plus tinned and frozen veg are really budget friendly. Sometimes, I just use microwave rice instead of making my own, and fresh pasta cooks faster than dried. It's all about making meal prepping work for you and your current lifestyle, rather than letting it rule your life.

I hope these tips help you to find meal prepping a lot less daunting and that you can implement at least a few of them into your daily routine.

My Kitchen Staples

These are the ingredients that I buy and use all the time. You'll find a lot of them in many of my recipes, they are all pretty budget friendly, and they are all really versatile! I've also added some tips and tricks on how to store them, to help reduce waste and save money.

MEAT

Lean cuts

I always pick the leaner cuts of meat, like 5% fat mince, bacon or pork medallions, and chicken breast rather than thighs.

Larger joints

Sometimes I do use fattier pieces of meat like pork or lamb shoulder, but I do trim a lot of the fat off. I find the flavours in the dishes more than make up for a little bit of lost fat!

Chicken thighs

I cut off the fat, but I do like to use bone-in thighs where possible for extra flavour.

Cured meats

I use streaky bacon or chorizo in small quantities to enhance flavour in many dishes.

FRUITS AND VEGETABLES

Salad

I always have the ingredients for the most basic salad on hand: lettuce, tomatoes, bell peppers and cucumber. A simple dressing of lemon juice and salt brings them to life.

Spinach

This high-protein veggie is great for bulking out meals. Because it cooks down so much, you can pack a lot in. It's also lovely in salads! Store in a bag lined with kitchen towel to keep longer.

Cauliflower

I grate raw cauliflower into rice dishes to bulk out the meal and add more fibre. I prefer homemade cauliflower rice to the ready-made packets and you won't taste it in your dishes.

Courgette

Another versatile veggie I couldn't live without! As well as pan frying and roasting, I grate courgette into lots of dishes – including risotto, orzo and recipes with minced meat to keep them juicy – as it takes on the flavour of what you're cooking.

Butternut squash

This is delicious roasted as a side dish and when cooked and blended into a purée it makes any dish super creamy, without the need for extra cream, milk or cheese.

Potatoes

Again, these can last a while when stored properly (in a cool dark place, NOT with your onions) and sweet potatoes are always useful to add a bit of variety into your cooking. There's lots of ways to use up old potatoes in this book too!

Aromatics

Onions, garlic, ginger, and chilli are all important in the kitchen. The great thing about onions and garlic is that they last for months when stored properly in a cool, dark spot. I am partial to shallots for a sweeter flavour. I also keep some diced onions, shallots, and chopped garlic in the freezer, alongside ginger and chilli which can be grated straight in from frozen.

Fresh herbs and spices

I grow fresh herbs in my kitchen and garden, but when I buy them from the supermarket, I store them in the fridge in a jar of water which I change every 3-4 days for freshness.

FISH

Oily fish

I try to have oily fish like salmon or mackerel at least once a week. Salmon is very versatile because of its firmness; you can treat it like meat. It also doesn't lose flavour when frozen unlike some white fish, and can be cooked from frozen, so it's great to have on hand. I get it cheaper by buying a half or whole side, then portioning and freezing it myself.

White fish

I find white fish is better and has more flavour when bought pre-frozen, as opposed to freezing it yourself. Cod and haddock are always favourites, even for fussy eaters, and if you like those and haven't tried hake yet, you're missing out!

Shellfish

I always have a bag of frozen prawns on hand too, as they defrost really quickly and provide a great source of protein.

Tinned fish

Tuna and mackerel are some of my staples; they can be used in lunches or dinners for a quick and easy meal.

DAIRY

Milk

I buy skimmed milk and find this an easy swap as for me it doesn't change the flavour or texture of my dishes too much. I buy the long-life version for when I need milk in a pinch!

Cheese

Mozzarella, cheddar and parmesan are my go-to cheeses and I often opt for the reduced fat versions but like to buy good quality as they have better meltability. I only buy the 30% reduced fat versions (not 50%) as I find this gives a great balance between the fat/calories and taste/texture.

Cream cheese

I usually go for the lighter version as it contains slightly fewer calories and is often higher in protein. Again, if you buy good quality cream cheese the difference in texture is minimal compared to the full-fat version.

Greek yoghurt

I always have a big tub of 0% fat Greek yoghurt in my fridge! Make sure you buy Greek yoghurt (not 'Greek style') as it has a thicker consistency. It's high in protein and a versatile ingredient; I add it to flatbread dough, sauces, quiche fillings, dipping sauces, and enjoy it as a snack or dessert too.

Coconut milk and yoghurt

Although not technically dairy, coconut products can be used in similar ways. Tinned coconut milk is high in calories and fat, even the lighter version, so I substitute this with a combination of coconut milk drink and coconut yoghurt. Coconut milk drink is thinner than tinned coconut milk but adds so much flavour. Coconut yoghurt is the thickening element. You can find high protein 0% fat coconut yoghurts in most supermarkets now, and they have a fairly long shelf life too.

CUPBOARD ESSENTIALS

Tomatoes

I always make sure to have tinned chopped tomatoes, passata and purée in the cupboard. I do think that the better-quality versions of these can make all the difference to a recipe!

Beans

Beans can help to bulk out any meal and are an excellent source of protein.

Tinned or jarred veg

I often buy cuisine-specific ingredients in tins or jars – such as bamboo shoots, water chestnuts, or jalapeños – so I can always whip up something interesting in a pinch! Roasted red peppers and olives are great additions to sauces and salads too, and a little goes a long way.

Rice and pasta

I have a slight obsession with buying interesting shapes of pasta! The basis of many meals, these staples are easy to cook and ideal when you don't have potatoes or lots of fresh veg around. I do cheat and buy microwavable packets of rice sometimes for those lazy days!

Stock

I often use wine stock pots, and fish or lamb stock cubes are great for adding extra flavour to dishes when you don't have homemade stock. When time and ingredients allow (usually after making a roast) I make my own chicken stock simply by throwing chicken bones and some veg peelings into the slow cooker, covering them with water and simmering overnight. You can then strain the stock, portion and freeze for later use.

Soy sauce

I always keep both light and dark soy sauces in the cupboard, as it's useful in lots of recipes alongside the usual Asian-inspired dishes. Light soy sauce is saltier, while dark soy sauce is thicker and sweeter. It goes well with red meats and makes a great base for a dipping sauce.

Nuts and seeds

I always have cashew nuts, hazelnuts, pine nuts, and sesame seeds in. I like them sprinkled on top of a dish as well as in cooking, like pine nuts in pesto, or hazelnuts in stuffing.

Honey

I couldn't live without honey in my kitchen! Maple syrup and agave nectar are good substitutes if you don't eat honey. It can thicken sauces, create a sticky glaze, add subtle sweetness, and improve vegetables: honey roasted veg or salad topped with a Dijon mustard and honey dressing are unmatched!

Bicarbonate of soda

This is best for breaking down foods; I add it to the water when boiling potatoes for roasties, which helps them fluff up really well. It's also great for tenderising meat (even cheaper cuts) when you're cooking them quickly in something like a stir fry.

Cornflour

My usual choice of thickening agent. Just mix 1 tablespoon with 1-2 tablespoons of cold water to make a smooth paste, then add this to your dish which will quickly thicken when heated.

Jarred sauces

Pesto, mustards, and harissa paste are all things I try to keep handy for an easy way to add flavour to a dish.

Mayonnaise

I always use the light version, as I'm often mixing it with other things so the flavour and texture doesn't feel compromised.

Balsamic vinegar

Vinegars add amazing flavour and balance to so many dishes. I use balsamic in lots of different recipes, including anything Italian-inspired, or BBQ flavoured. It's also lovely reduced down into a thick glaze, and drizzled over salads or roasted vegetables.

OILS AND FATS

Cooking oil spray

I tend to use this in most of my cooking and I prefer the actual oil rather than the '1 calorie' cooking sprays. The oil doesn't spoil your cookware like the emulsified cooking sprays can, and a little goes a long way as you generally need half as much compared to the cooking spray.

Olive oil

I usually go for olive oil as it's so versatile, great for dressing salads or veggies, and the smoke point is similar to other cooking oils so you can cook with it too, even in an air fryer.

Butter

I also like to use light butter in some recipes. You don't need much but it can help to add that extra flavour and texture that you would otherwise miss. Don't be afraid of butter!

Notes on the Recipes

APPLIANCES

I developed all these recipes using a fan assisted oven and gas hob. If you like to use an air fryer when cooking, look out for this symbol in the notes at the bottom of each page; if it's there, you'll find air fryer cooking instructions within that recipe. I have included some slow cooker recipes in this book too, but you can substitute a slow cooker for a heavy saucepan with a lid on the hob, or a Dutch oven with a lid in the oven. I have also used a blender/food processor in a few of the recipes, but I have suggested alternatives where possible in case you don't have access to one of these. One thing I would recommend buying though is an immersion hand blender, which are the cheapest blenders to buy and can be used for many different processes.

COOKWARE

Aside from the usual pots, pans, chopping boards and knives, a few things I would highly recommend are a hob-oven casserole dish with a lid, scales and measuring spoons, a juicer, and a potato ricer. The casserole dish is a worthy investment as they are very robust, last a long time, and fit in a large amount of food, so they are perfect for batch cooking or cooking for families, and are of course very versatile as they will work on the hob or in an oven. Scales and measuring spoons are important to make sure you have the perfect balance of ingredients. A juicer and a potato ricer are optional extras, but the amount of juice I can extract from citrus with a juicer reduces so much waste, and a potato ricer creates the fluffiest mashed potatoes with minimal effort.

COOKING TIMES AND TEMPERATURES

Be wary that cooking times and temperatures will vary slightly depending on a multitude of factors; your ingredients may be slightly bigger or smaller than specified in the recipe, all ovens and hobs are different so you may need to adjust accordingly; and even the quality of your ingredients may affect things (for example, lower quality meat may dry out faster and have a shorter cooking time, vegetables may contain more water and need longer to cook down). I would always recommend checking the dish 5-10 minutes before the end of the suggested cooking time to assess it from there.

CALORIES

The calorie information for each recipe refers to a single serving and does not include any sides or serving suggestions. You'll find that calorie counts can vary massively depending on the brand of ingredients used, so the most reliable way to check is to look at the packaging of the ingredient you are actually using. I often shop around to find lower calorie versions of ingredients as they can vary so much. Please remember that this information is meant as guidance only.

NUTRITIONAL INFORMATION

Please note that I am not a certified nutritionist; these nutritional values are based on the packaging of the ingredients I used to create each recipe. I personally aim to include lots of fibre and protein in my meals, balanced with fats and carbs, but everyone's requirements are different, and this is not meant to replace dietary advice from your own qualified doctor, dietitian, or nutritionist.

FREEZING

I have marked a number of recipes in this book as suitable for freezing with this symbol to help you with preparing meals in advance and batch cooking.

MEAL PREP MONDAYS

On Mondays, we meal prep! All these meals are ones you can easily batch cook with little to no extra prep time, meaning you can stash away the leftovers in the fridge or freezer for those evenings when things don't quite go to plan, or to use for lunches. It's all about working smarter, not harder, and getting your week off to a strong start when you're feeling most motivated!

Crispy Potato Topped Chicken & Chorizo Bake

PREP TIME: 10 MINUTES | COOK TIME: 55 MINUTES | SERVES: 4

The creamy, smoky filling in this dish complements the crispy golden topping so well, and makes for a delicious, comforting meal the whole family will love!

INGREDIENTS

500g potatoes, thinly sliced
75g chorizo, diced
1 white onion, finely diced
6 cloves of garlic, grated
1 red bell pepper, diced
400g chicken breast, diced
2 tbsp smoked paprika
2 tbsp dried oregano
1 tsp salt
1 tsp black pepper
1 tsp dried thyme
400g tinned chopped tomatoes
2 tbsp tomato purée
75g light cream cheese
75g cheddar, grated
1 tbsp cornflour

METHOD

1. First, submerge the sliced potatoes in a bowl of boiling water and set aside while you cook the filling (this is going to help them get extra crispy later!).

2. Fry the chorizo and onion in a large pan until the onion has softened a little, then stir in the garlic, red pepper, and chicken. Add half the smoked paprika, oregano, salt and black pepper along with all the thyme and fry until the chicken is fully cooked through.

3. Add the chopped tomatoes, tomato purée, cream cheese and cheddar to the pan. Mix well until everything is combined, then pour the mixture into an ovenproof dish.

4. Drain the sliced potatoes and dry them off with a clean tea towel or kitchen roll. Toss the potatoes with some cooking oil spray, the cornflour, and the remaining paprika, oregano, salt and black pepper until fully coated.

5. Layer the potatoes on top of the chicken mixture in the dish, overlapping them but only slightly which will allow them to cook evenly and crisp up beautifully.

6. Spray the top of the bake with a little more oil for good measure and bake for around 40 minutes at 180°c until the potatoes are cooked through and golden on top.

7. This is perfect served with lots of green veg on the side; I like griddled tenderstem broccoli or asparagus, spring greens cooked with lemon, or some steamed green beans or peas.

Tips: I love to swap the cheddar for a smoked cheese as it adds a lovely depth of flavour to this bake. It can be difficult to get hold of, but I always pick up reduced-fat chorizo if I can!

CALS:	CARBS:	FAT:	PROTEIN:	DIETARY:
467	35G	15.16G	45.6G	GF

Creamy Honey Mustard Chicken

PREP TIME: 5 MINUTES | COOK TIME: 25 MINUTES | SERVES: 4

This easy, comforting recipe is done in one pan and just 30 minutes. It can be served with so many different sides too; you could have it every day of the week and still feel as though you were having something new each day!

INGREDIENTS

400g chicken breast, sliced
1 tbsp plain flour
2 tsp smoked paprika
2 shallots, finely diced
4 cloves of garlic, grated
2 tsp light butter
300ml chicken stock
2 tbsp honey
2 tsp Dijon mustard
1 tbsp wholegrain mustard
1 tsp dried oregano
1 tsp dried basil
1 tsp dried thyme
½ lemon, juiced
100g light cream cheese
50g parmesan, finely grated

METHOD

1. Toss the sliced chicken in the flour and half the smoked paprika with salt and black pepper to taste. Mix thoroughly until coated.

2. Fry the shallot and garlic on a low heat with the light butter and some cooking oil spray. Once softened, add the chicken to the pan and cook on a medium heat until beginning to brown.

3. Now add the stock, honey, Dijon mustard, wholegrain mustard, remaining smoked paprika, and the oregano, basil and thyme. Simmer for 10 minutes or so, until the liquid reduces.

4. Stir in the lemon juice, cream cheese and parmesan and keep stirring to mix everything together on a low heat until the sauce has thickened.

5. Season to taste with salt if needed (this is unlikely due to the stock and parmesan) and pepper; I like to use a mix of white and black pepper for this dish.

6. Once the chicken is cooked through and the sauce is the right consistency, there are so many ways to serve this! It's lovely over boiled rice, mixed with pasta, on a jacket potato or with other potato sides such as air fried, roast or mashed potatoes. I think it goes perfectly with some green veg like green beans and tenderstem broccoli too.

Tips: A small white onion would work instead of the shallots if you don't have any; I just love the sweetness of shallots in this dish. If using bottled lemon juice instead of fresh, you'll need a couple of tablespoons.

CALS:	CARBS:	FAT:	PROTEIN:	
272	12.4G	11.1G	30.4G	

Red Thai Chicken Orzo

Orzo works so well with a creamy sauce, and with its rice-like appearance and texture, it's perfect for soaking up all the delicious flavours that red Thai curry has to offer!

INGREDIENTS

400g chicken breast, thinly sliced

½ tsp bicarbonate of soda

1 tbsp cornflour

2 tbsp light soy sauce

3 tbsp red Thai curry paste

2 shallots, finely diced

4 cloves of garlic, grated

1 tsp grated ginger

1 tsp lemongrass paste

½-1 red chilli, finely diced (optional – or Thai chilli if you're brave!)

200g orzo

350ml chicken stock

250ml coconut milk from a carton

200g tenderstem broccoli, trimmed

1 red bell pepper, sliced

50g fat-free coconut yoghurt or Icelandic style yoghurt

Handful of fresh coriander, to serve (optional)

METHOD

1. Add the sliced chicken to a bowl with the bicarbonate of soda, cornflour and soy sauce. Mix thoroughly, then leave to sit for at least 10 minutes while you prepare the other ingredients.

2. Fry the red Thai curry paste in the large pan with the shallots, garlic, ginger, lemongrass paste, and chilli if using.

3. After about 1 minute, add the chicken to the pan and fry until it has some colour on the edges.

4. Add the orzo, mix well to coat in all the juices and let it fry for a minute or so. Pour in the chicken stock and coconut milk, then simmer for around 10 minutes, stirring often.

5. If you find the sauce is becoming too dry before the orzo is fully cooked, just add extra splashes of stock and/or coconut milk while it simmers.

6. Once the orzo is almost cooked through, stir in the broccoli and red pepper, add the coconut yoghurt for extra creaminess, and season to taste with salt and/or sweetener if you think it needs either or both. Simmer until everything is just tender.

7. I also like to stir in some fresh coriander and serve the orzo with sliced fresh chilli on top, but both of these are optional!

Tips: It's important to buy the coconut milk drink (in a carton, found with the milk alternatives in supermarkets) rather than coconut milk (in a tin, found on the world foods aisle) for this recipe. This is also delicious with fish like prawns or salmon instead of the chicken!

CALS:	CARBS:	FAT:	PROTEIN:	DIETARY:	
398	47.9G	5.1G	42.9G	DF (IF USING COCONUT YOGHURT)	

Cheeseburger Meatball Bake

PREP TIME: 10 MINUTES | COOK TIME: 25 MINUTES | SERVES: 4

Minced beef can get a bit boring, but not with this recipe! We all love a cheeseburger, and this has all those signature flavours packed into a simple, family-friendly bake.

INGREDIENTS

500g lean beef mince

4 tsp smoked paprika

3 tsp onion granules

2 tsp garlic granules

½ tsp mustard powder

1 tsp black pepper

1 beef stock cube, crumbled

400g tinned chopped tomatoes

1 tsp English mustard

100g Red Leicester cheese, grated

TO SERVE (OPTIONAL)

½ small white onion, finely diced

2 gherkins, finely diced

METHOD

1. Mix the beef mince with half the smoked paprika, 1 teaspoon each of the onion and garlic granules, and all the mustard powder, black pepper, and stock cube.

2. Roll the mince mixture into meatballs. This amount should make 16-20 meatballs, depending on how big you make them.

3. Fry the meatballs in a pan until browned on all sides and almost cooked through, which should take about 10 minutes. You can also air fry them for about 8 minutes at 180°c.

4. Combine the chopped tomatoes, remaining smoked paprika, onion and garlic granules, and English mustard in a baking dish. Mix well, then season to taste with salt and pepper.

5. Place your meatballs into the tomato sauce and top with the grated cheese. Bake in the oven at 180°c for 15 minutes, until the meatballs are fully cooked through, the sauce is bubbling, and the cheese has melted. If you have a big enough air fryer, you can cook this in there too; remove the basket and use like an ovenproof dish for about 10 minutes at 180°c.

6. To serve, scatter the dish with the finely diced onion and gherkins, if using. You could also add your choice of sauce: try burger sauce, mustard or ketchup!

Tips: I make my own lighter burger sauce to drizzle over this dish, by mixing 4 tablespoons of light mayo and 2 tablespoons of fat-free French dressing with 1 teaspoon of paprika, half a teaspoon each of sweetener and English mustard, and finely diced shallots and gherkins (about a tablespoon of each).

CALS:	CARBS:	FAT:	PROTEIN:	DIETARY:
326	5.7G	15.1G	41.6G	GF (CHECK THE MUSTARD)

Slow Cooker BBQ Pulled Pork

PREP TIME: 15 MINUTES | COOK TIME: 6 HOURS | SERVES: 8

This is such a versatile meal that feels like it's making itself! I like it in a sandwich, on pasta, with rice or chips… there are endless ways to enjoy this, and if you can't quite find enough ways to eat it, this pulled pork freezes really well too.

INGREDIENTS

I pork shoulder (approx. 800g)

3 tbsp smoked paprika

2 tbsp paprika

I tbsp onion granules

I tbsp garlic granules

3 tsp salt

2 tsp white pepper

I white onion

2 red onions

4 cloves of garlic

400g tinned chopped tomatoes

85ml balsamic vinegar

I tbsp Worcestershire Sauce

6 tbsp sweetener

3 tbsp BBQ seasoning

I tsp mustard powder

I tsp cayenne pepper

METHOD

1. Trim the fat off your pork shoulder and cut into 3-4 smaller chunks.

2. Combine I tablespoon each of the smoked paprika and paprika with the onion and garlic granules, 2 teaspoons of the salt, and all the white pepper.

3. Sprinkle your spice mix all over the pork shoulder and rub in so each piece is well coated. Spray a large frying pan with oil and sear the meat on all sides (do this in batches if your pan isn't big enough, so that you don't overcrowd the pan).

4. Once they are browned on all sides, transfer the pieces of pork to your slow cooker.

5. Meanwhile, peel the onions and garlic, chop them roughly and then blend with the chopped tomatoes in a food processor or blender.

6. Add the tomato mixture to the pan you seared the pork in, collecting all the flavour and cooking off the onion and garlic slightly, then pour it into the slow cooker.

7. Now add the balsamic vinegar, Worcestershire Sauce, sweetener, BBQ seasoning, mustard powder, cayenne pepper, and the remaining smoked paprika, paprika and salt.

8. Put the slow cooker on low to cook for a minimum of 6 hours – anywhere up to 9 hours will also work!

9. For the last hour of cooking, I like to shred the meat, turn the slow cooker up to high and leave the lid off while I prep my sides.

10. I like to serve this pulled pork with wholemeal rolls, chunky air fried potato wedges, salad and coleslaw.

Tips: I often prep this the night before I want to cook it and put everything in the fridge overnight, then dump it in the slow cooker in the morning and just switch it on!

CALS:	CARBS:	FAT:	PROTEIN:	DIETARY:	
280	9.1G	13.7G	26.8G	GF, DF (CHECK THE BBQ SEASONING)	

Slow Cooker Turkish Lamb

PREP TIME: 20 MINUTES | COOK TIME: 6 HOURS | SERVES: 8

This rich casserole is inspired by a dish I've had many times while on holiday in Turkey. It works as a cosy winter warmer or as a lighter summer dinner, depending on what you serve it with.

INGREDIENTS

2 aubergines, diced

2 tbsp smoked paprika

1 tsp salt

1kg diced lamb

1 tsp ground cumin

400g fresh tomatoes, roughly chopped

400g tinned chopped tomatoes

1 green bell pepper, diced

1 red bell pepper, diced

1 tbsp Turkish red pepper paste

1 tbsp tomato purée

1 tbsp dried oregano

2 tsp black pepper

2 lamb stock cubes

250ml boiling water

40g mozzarella, grated (optional)

METHOD

1. Toss the diced aubergine in half the smoked paprika, the salt, and some cooking oil spray, then air fry or bake for 20-25 minutes at 180°c until just beginning to brown and soften.

2. Meanwhile, coat the diced lamb in the remaining smoked paprika, cumin, and a pinch of salt and pepper.

3. Brown the lamb in a pan, working in batches so that you don't overcrowd the pan, then transfer it to the slow cooker when sealed on all sides.

4. Add the baked aubergine, fresh and tinned tomatoes, bell peppers, Turkish red pepper paste, tomato purée, oregano, black pepper, stock cubes, and boiling water to the slow cooker.

5. Give the mixture a good stir and then place the lid on the slow cooker and cook on low for 6-8 hours. Once the lamb is cooked and completely tender, shred the meat.

6. I like to leave the lid off and turn the heat up to high for the last hour of cooking, so the sauce reduces and thickens slightly.

7. This step is optional, but I like to put my portion into an ovenproof dish and top it with grated mozzarella, then bake until golden and bubbling on top.

8. I love this lamb dish with rice (I always have half white rice, half cauliflower rice), salad and sometimes a few chips too – just like holidays in Turkey!

Tips: You can swap Turkish red pepper paste for tomato purée and extra smoked paprika, or harissa paste. You can use 2 tins of chopped tomatoes if you don't have fresh ones, though I love the flavour from adding fresh tomatoes as well as tinned, and I always use vine tomatoes for the best flavour.

CALS:	CARBS:	FAT:	PROTEIN:	DIETARY: GF (CHECK THE STOCK)
327	10.7G	9.1G	48.3G	DF (SKIP THE CHEESE)

Lamb and Rosemary Bolognese

PREP TIME: 10 MINUTES | COOK TIME: 50 MINUTES | SERVES: 4

We all love a Bolognese and this is a slightly elevated version of the dish we all know and love, perfect for mixing up the mundane meals that we repeat week on week!

INGREDIENTS

1 white onion
2 carrots
2 celery stalks
6 cloves of garlic
500g lean lamb mince (10% fat)
50g tomato purée
50ml skimmed milk
250ml red wine stock
400g tinned chopped tomatoes
2 tbsp balsamic vinegar
1 lamb stock cube
1 tbsp dried oregano
2 sprigs of fresh rosemary

METHOD

1. Start by finely dicing the onion, carrots, celery and garlic – personally I like to throw them all in a food processor for speed and ease!

2. Put the lamb mince into a cold pan (this is important to get tender meat later) with some cooking oil spray. Turn the heat to medium and stir until the mince is beginning to brown.

3. Add your finely diced vegetables to the pan and let them sweat down. Once they start to soften, add the tomato purée and stir until it changes to a deeper red colour.

4. Add the milk, red wine stock, chopped tomatoes, balsamic vinegar, lamb stock cube, oregano and fresh rosemary to the pan. Stir and then leave to simmer for around 40 minutes, checking occasionally, until the liquid has reduced and the sauce has thickened.

5. If you have time to simmer the Bolognese for 1-2 hours at this stage, even better! You'll get an extra depth of flavour this way; just add an extra 200ml or so of red wine stock.

6. Once the sauce is nice and thick, season to taste with salt and black pepper. I usually find that it doesn't really need salt, but I love plenty of black pepper!

7. Serve the Bolognese with whatever pasta you like best; it's great with the classic spaghetti, but I also like it with a tubed pasta like penne or rigatoni, or shell pasta like conchiglie, which all collect the sauce really well. I also like to sprinkle some cheese on top; in the winter I go classic with grated parmesan, but in the summer I like it with crumbled feta!

Tips: If you can't get fresh rosemary, substitute it with 2 teaspoons of dried rosemary. If you can't get red wine stock pots, you can use lamb stock and add a splash of red wine if you like!

CALS:	CARBS:	FAT:	PROTEIN:	DIETARY: GF (CHECK THE STOCK)
328	22.3G	14.4G	33.1G	DF (SKIP THE MILK)

Pesto Fish Pie

PREP TIME: 15 MINUTES | COOK TIME: 35 MINUTES | SERVES: 6

An Italian twist on this comforting classic, perfect for preparing in advance and freezing for those nights when you just can't be bothered to cook!

INGREDIENTS

4 fillets of salmon

1kg potatoes, peeled and diced

300ml skimmed milk

1 tbsp cornflour, mixed to a paste with cold water

3 tbsp light cream cheese

3 tbsp light pesto

1 tbsp dried oregano

2 tsp dried basil

½ tsp dried thyme

1 lemon, zested and juiced

300g cooked prawns

150g spinach

METHOD

1. Season the salmon with salt and pepper, then bake in the oven at 180°c for 12-15 minutes, or air fry for 10 minutes. Set aside to cool before flaking into chunks, removing the skin.

2. Meanwhile, boil the diced potatoes until softened, then drain and leave to cool with a tea towel over the top to keep the steam in. Set aside 1 tablespoon of the cream cheese and 2 tablespoons of the pesto to use later for the mash.

3. To make the sauce, warm the milk in a pan and then add the cornflour paste. Whisk until beginning to thicken, then stir in all the remaining ingredients including the flaked salmon.

4. Season the pie filling to taste with salt and pepper, then transfer it to an ovenproof dish and allow to cool slightly while you make the topping.

5. Mash the potatoes (I recommend a potato ricer for the fluffiest mash!) and then fold in the cream cheese and pesto you set aside earlier. Season to taste with salt and pepper if desired. You can also add a splash of milk to thin the mash if it's too thick.

6. Spoon the creamy pesto mash over your pie filling and smooth out the top with the back of a spoon or a fork.

7. Bake the pie in the oven at 180°c for about 15 minutes, until the top begins to turn golden brown.

8. Leave it to rest for 10 minutes before cutting into the pie and serving. I like mine with some tenderstem broccoli done in the griddle pan with lemon juice, olive oil and salt.

Tips: Make sure your filling has cooled before you add the mash to the dish, and leave your pie to stand for 10 minutes before portioning it – this should mean it doesn't fall apart when serving.

CALS:	CARBS:	FAT:	PROTEIN:	DIETARY:
364	40.7G	6.8G	32.2G	GF

Arrabiata Al Forno

PREP TIME: 5 MINUTES | COOK TIME: 30 MINUTES | SERVES: 4

Pasta in spicy Italian tomato sauce is a classic for a reason, but when you add cheese and bake it, this dish just gets better!

INGREDIENTS

1 tsp light butter

1 tsp olive oil

½ tsp chilli flakes

2 red onions, diced

240g dried pasta (penne works well)

6 cloves of garlic, grated

600g cherry tomatoes

100g tomato purée

50ml balsamic vinegar

2 tbsp dried oregano

1 tbsp dried basil

5g each fresh basil and parsley (optional)

100g mozzarella, grated

30g parmesan, grated

METHOD

1. Heat the butter and olive oil in a pan, add the chilli flakes and stir for a minute or so, then stir in the red onion and cook until beginning to soften.

2. Meanwhile, cook your pasta in heavily salted boiling water until al dente.

3. Stir the grated garlic into the onions and cook until the raw edge has gone. Add the cherry tomatoes and tomato purée to the pan. Cook down until the tomatoes begin to soften, enough that you can squish them with the back of your spoon.

4. Add the balsamic vinegar, oregano and basil to the tomato sauce and mix everything together. If it starts to seem dry at any point, stir in a splash of boiling water.

5. Once the pasta is cooked, drain it and reserve the cooking water, then tip the cooked pasta into the sauce. Stir or toss with a splash of the cooking water to coat the pasta.

6. Add the fresh herbs if using, then season to taste with salt, black pepper (I like a lot in this!) and maybe sweetener if you feel it needs it.

7. Transfer the pasta and sauce to an ovenproof dish, top with the mozzarella and parmesan cheese, then bake for 10-15 minutes at 190°c until golden on top.

8. This goes perfectly with a simple salad dressed in lemon juice and olive oil, or a rocket, parmesan and tomato salad dressed in balsamic vinegar.

Tips: Add more chilli flakes in Step 1 if you like a bit more spice! When using fresh tomatoes, tomatoes on the vine are always best as they have the most flavour.

CALS:	CARBS:	FAT:	PROTEIN:	DIETARY:
464	62.6G	10.8G	18.3G	VEGGIE

Roasted Veggie Enchiladas

PREP TIME: 15 MINUTES | COOK TIME: 40 MINUTES | SERVES: 4

Who needs meat when these veggie enchiladas pack in so much flavour? This is a great way to get fussy eaters to eat some veg and it's a very 'hands off' meal too. Exactly what we need on busy weeknights!

INGREDIENTS

4 tsp chilli powder

2 tbsp smoked paprika

1 tbsp ground cumin

1 tbsp dried oregano

2 tsp paprika

2 tsp onion granules

2 tsp garlic granules

1 tsp ground coriander

½ tsp white pepper

1 tsp salt

1 butternut squash, diced into 1cm chunks

1 yellow bell pepper, roughly diced

1 red bell pepper, roughly diced

2 red onions, roughly chopped

2 courgettes, roughly diced

150g cherry tomatoes

250ml passata

1 lime, juiced

100ml vegetable stock

1 tin of sweetcorn, drained

4 tortilla wraps

100g cheese of your choice, grated

Fresh coriander, to serve

METHOD

1. Set aside half the chilli powder and smoked paprika for later, then combine all the remaining spices and salt to make your enchilada seasoning. Lay all the prepared vegetables on a large tray or two, making sure they are in a single layer.

2. Spray the vegetables with oil, cover with the enchilada seasoning and then massage it in so that everything is thoroughly coated.

3. Roast the spiced veg in the oven at 180°c for about 30 minutes, shaking the tray halfway through, until everything is softened and beginning to char on the edges a little. You can also air fry the veg if your air fryer is big enough; just keep stirring to make sure it cooks evenly.

4. Meanwhile, prep your other ingredients and make the enchilada sauce. Mix the passata with the lime juice, stock, remaining smoked paprika and chilli powder, then set aside.

5. Once the vegetables are ready, mix them with the sweetcorn and then divide the veggie mixture evenly between your tortilla wraps. Roll the wraps up to enclose the filling.

6. Pour half of the enchilada sauce into an ovenproof dish (or your air fryer without the basket) and then add the rolled-up wraps, nestled tightly together, with the seams facing down.

7. Top with the remaining enchilada sauce and sprinkle the grated cheese on top. Oven bake for about 10 minutes at 180°c just until the cheese is melted and the edges of the tortillas begin to brown and crisp up.

8. Serve your enchiladas with some fresh coriander on top and lime wedges for squeezing over on the side. I love these with spicy rice or potato wedges, a side salad, and some fat-free Greek yoghurt (it tastes just like sour cream but is higher in protein and lower in fat!).

Tips: Swap the fresh lime for lemon in a pinch, or if using bottled lime juice, use about 40ml. I like using a spicy cheese on these, but cheddar, Red Leicester, or even a smoked cheese work well!

CALS:	CARBS:	FAT:	PROTEIN:	DIETARY: **VEGAN**	
375	43.3G	11.8G	16.5G	(SKIP THE CHEESE OR USE PLANT-BASED)	

ONE POT TUESDAYS

Why do Tuesdays always seem like such hectic days? These recipes are all about simplicity – keeping everything in one pot, with minimal fuss – to save on the washing up and stop you from standing over the stove while you're busy with other things.

Paella

PREP TIME: 10 MINUTES | COOK TIME: 45 MINUTES | SERVES: 4

This is a classic you'll come back to again and again. It's easy to make (definitely easier than you think!) and a crowd pleaser every single time! It's by no means a traditional paella, but it's packed with Spanish flavours and perfect for anyone on a budget.

INGREDIENTS

400g (3-4) chicken breasts, diced

3 tbsp smoked paprika

8 cloves of garlic, minced

2 white onions, finely diced

100g chorizo, diced

2 red bell peppers, diced

300g cherry tomatoes, halved

1 tsp ground turmeric

2 tbsp tomato purée

200g paella rice

1.2 litres stock (preferably chicken)

100g frozen peas or green beans

10g fresh parsley, finely chopped

1 large fresh lemon, sliced into wedges

METHOD

1. Toss the diced chicken in 1 tablespoon of the smoked paprika, all the fresh garlic and a sprinkle of salt, then leave in the fridge while you prep other ingredients. The longer the better here but 10-20 minutes will still do the trick in a pinch!

2. Fry the onions and chorizo in cooking oil spray on a low-medium heat. Once the onions begin to soften, and the chorizo has released its oils, add the marinated chicken.

3. Cook for a few minutes until the chicken is sealed and almost cooked through, then add the red pepper and cherry tomatoes (I like to save a handful of the tomatoes for later).

4. When they begin to soften, stir in the remaining smoked paprika, turmeric, tomato purée, and rice. Allow the rice to toast slightly and become coated in all the juices from the pan.

5. Once the rice is coated, add about one third of your stock (enough to just cover everything in the pan). Give it a stir and bring up to the boil, then pop a lid on the pan and lower the heat.

6. Leave for around 5-10 minutes to simmer on a low heat, then check all the liquid has been absorbed. Give it a stir, add more stock, and repeat the process.

7. Keep doing this until you either run out of stock, or your rice is fully cooked through, which should take around 3-4 stages. You may need more or less stock than you have prepared, so keep checking your rice as it cooks.

8. Once the rice is cooked, take the lid off, turn the heat up, and add the frozen peas or beans. If you kept back some tomatoes, add those here too.

9. Stir the paella on a high heat until it becomes less wet, and the peas are cooked through. I like to serve it with a sprinkling of fresh parsley, and some fresh lemon wedges for squeezing over. It's lovely with a simple salad dressed with lemon juice and salt on the side too.

Tips: I like to use homemade stock where possible but if not, stock pots give a richer flavour compared to stock cubes. Make sure you use enough stock pots or cubes for the amount of liquid in the recipe. You can get a 'light' version of chorizo, which I like to use when I can find it.

CALS:	CARBS:	FAT:	PROTEIN:	DIETARY:	
475	29.7G	8.4G	50.1G	DF, GF (CHECK THE STOCK CUBE)	

Lemon Chicken and Halloumi Traybake

PREP TIME: 10 MINUTES | COOK TIME: 50 MINUTES | SERVES: 4

Don't we all love a 'throw it together' meal? This delicious dish reminds me of holidays abroad thanks to the bright, lemony flavour. No need to prep sides with this one: you've got your protein, fats, carbs, and fibre all in one pan!

INGREDIENTS

400-500g (about 4) skinless and boneless chicken thighs

500-600g new potatoes

1 lemon, halved (plus extra to serve if you like)

6 cloves of garlic, whole and unpeeled

2 tbsp dried oregano

1 tbsp dried parsley

1 tbsp smoked paprika

1 tsp dried dill

300g tenderstem broccoli

200g halloumi, sliced into 8 pieces

2 tbsp honey

5g fresh parsley and/or dill (optional)

METHOD

1. Preheat your oven to 180°c fan and prep all your ingredients, then put the chicken thighs, potatoes, lemon halves, and garlic cloves into a roasting tin.

2. Spray all over with olive oil, then sprinkle over the oregano, parsley, smoked paprika, and dill. You can also add salt here but be wary that the halloumi we add later is also salty!

3. Mix everything together with your hands and spread out in a single layer, making sure the lemon halves are cut side down in the tin.

4. Cover the tin with foil and oven bake at 180°c for around 20 minutes, then remove the foil and bake uncovered for another 20 minutes, until the potatoes are almost fork-tender, the chicken juices run clear, and the garlic is soft and squishy.

5. Remove the roasting tin from the oven, squeeze the garlic out of the skins, and squeeze over the roasted lemon. Mix everything together and spread flat again.

6. Place the tenderstem broccoli and halloumi on top of the traybake, then pop it back in the oven for another 10-15 minutes, until the broccoli is cooked and the halloumi is golden.

7. Drizzle the honey over the finished traybake and sprinkle the fresh herbs on top if using (a fresh version of any herbs used in the recipe works well). I sometimes like to add extra lemon slices or wedges too!

CALS:	CARBS:	FAT:	PROTEIN:	DIETARY:
471	26.5G	17.5G	23.6G	GF

Nacho Chicken Bake

PREP TIME: 10 MINUTES | COOK TIME: 35 MINUTES | SERVES: 4

Usually, you have nachos topped with chicken – here you have chicken topped with nachos! The tomato salsa-inspired sauce is a delicious base for the crunchy, cheesy chicken.

INGREDIENTS

900g tomatoes, diced

2 red bell peppers, diced

1 red onion, finely diced

6 cloves of garlic, roughly chopped

1 tbsp dried coriander leaf

2 tbsp smoked paprika

2 tsp dried oregano

3 tsp chilli powder

1 ½ tsp salt

1 tsp ground cumin

4 chicken breasts

100g cheddar, grated

30g tortilla chips, roughly crushed

TO SERVE (OPTIONAL)

Fresh lime wedges

Fresh coriander

Jalapeños

Guacamole

Fat-free Greek yoghurt

METHOD

1. In an ovenproof dish, mix the tomatoes, bell peppers, onion and garlic with the coriander, half the smoked paprika and oregano, 2 teaspoons of the chilli powder, and 1 teaspoon of the salt.

2. Mix the remaining smoked paprika, oregano, chilli powder, salt, and the cumin together. Rub this mixture all over the chicken breasts along with some cooking oil spray until fully coated.

3. Place the chicken breasts into the veggie mixture, cover the dish with foil and cook for 25-30 minutes in the oven at 180°c.

4. Remove the foil, spoon some of the veggie mixture over the chicken, then top with the grated cheese and crushed tortilla chips.

5. Bake uncovered in the oven for another 5-10 minutes, until the cheese has melted and the topping is extra golden and crunchy.

6. I love this dish with some fresh lime juice squeezed over, plus fresh coriander and jalapeños on top. I also love guacamole and fat-free Greek yoghurt (rather than sour cream) on the side. The whole thing goes really well with spiced rice or wedges and a big salad!

Tips: I prefer fresh vine tomatoes in this, but tinned chopped tomatoes will definitely work in a pinch. Spicy cheese works well on top of this dish if you want to try something different from cheddar! You can also make this recipe in the air fryer! Just add the ingredients in without the basket, cook for 20 minutes at first, then another 5 minutes once the cheese and chips have been added, all at 180°c.

CALS:	CARBS:	FAT:	PROTEIN:
412	17G	13.1G	55.1G

Moroccan Chicken

PREP TIME: 10 MINUTES | COOK TIME: 35 MINUTES | SERVES: 4

There are so many delicious flavours in this recipe – bright lemon, salty olives, sweet cinnamon and smoky paprika – and they all come together perfectly in one pot!

INGREDIENTS

2 tsp ground cinnamon
2 tsp ground coriander
2 tsp ground cumin
2 tsp smoked paprika
1 tsp ground turmeric
1 tsp ground ginger
1 tsp black pepper
6 chicken thighs
1 lemon, halved
2 tbsp plain flour
1 large white onion, diced
6 cloves of garlic, finely chopped
1 red bell pepper, sliced
400g tinned chopped tomatoes
200ml chicken stock
50g green olives, halved
5g fresh parsley
5g fresh coriander

METHOD

1. Combine all the ground spices and then rub half of this mixture into the chicken thighs and squeeze over the juice from the lemon.

2. Sprinkle the flour over the chicken thighs, making sure there is a thin even coating, then set aside.

3. Cut the juiced lemon into quarters and char them on all sides in a large pan for a few minutes, then remove and set aside.

4. Using the same pan, fry the spiced chicken thighs in some cooking oil spray until almost cooked through, which should take about 10 minutes, then remove and set aside.

5. Again using the same pan, fry the onion, garlic and red pepper until softened. Stir in the remaining spice mix and let it toast, darkening the colour slightly.

6. Now add the chopped tomatoes, chicken stock, and olives along with the charred lemon and chicken thighs from earlier.

7. Bring the sauce to the boil and then simmer for about 15 minutes until the liquid reduces to your preferred consistency.

8. Scatter the dish with fresh parsley and coriander to serve. I like to mix couscous directly into the sauce to soak up all the lovely flavours, but you can serve this separately (rice or potatoes go well with this dish too). I also love to have a fresh salad topped with pomegranate seeds and feta on the side!

Tips: If you don't mind bone-in chicken thighs, they will add even more flavour to your dish! Just remember to remove the skin before coating these in the spices. If you can get them, tinned cherry tomatoes are the best in this, adding a delicious sweetness.

CALS:	CARBS:	FAT:	PROTEIN:	DIETARY: DF
377	12.8G	16.3G	43.3G	GF (USE CORNFLOUR INSTEAD OF PLAIN)

Hawaiian Traybake

PREP TIME: 10 MINUTES | COOK TIME: 50 MINUTES | SERVES: 4

You're either going to love or hate this one… but if you're a fan of ham and pineapple on pizza, you're in for a treat!

INGREDIENTS

2 gammon steaks (about 500g), fat trimmed and cut into large chunks

500-600g new potatoes, quartered

200g fresh pineapple chunks

300g cherry tomatoes

2 tbsp honey

1 tbsp dried oregano

1 tbsp dried basil

1 tsp garlic granules

1 tsp black pepper

200g green beans, trimmed

125g ball of light mozzarella (optional)

Handful of fresh basil (optional)

METHOD

1. Preheat the oven to 180°c and prep all your ingredients, putting the gammon, potatoes, pineapple, and cherry tomatoes straight into a roasting tin.

2. Spray everything in the tin with oil, drizzle with the honey and season with the oregano, basil, garlic granules, and black pepper.

3. Mix everything together so that it's all well coated, then spread out evenly again (in a single layer where possible). Cover the tin with foil and bake for about 20 minutes.

4. Remove the foil, add the green beans and give everything a stir, then bake uncovered for another 15 minutes until the potatoes are tender.

5. You can also cook this in the air fryer for 20 minutes at 160°c, then give it a stir, add the beans and cook for another 10 minutes at 180°c.

6. If you like, tear the mozzarella over the traybake, nestle it in between everything, then pop the tin back into the oven for another 5-10 minutes, until the cheese is melted and golden brown on top.

7. I like to serve this with fresh basil on top, plus some extra veggies or salad on the side!

Tips: Make sure you have the pineapple and gammon touching in the tin before you pop it in the oven, so that the pineapple caramelises next to the meat and adds extra juicy flavour!

CALS:	CARBS:	FAT:	PROTEIN:	DIETARY:
393	30G	12.3G	37.5G	GF, DF (SKIP THE MOZZARELLA)

Piri Piri Salmon Traybake

PREP TIME: 10 MINUTES | COOK TIME: 45 MINUTES | SERVES: 4

We always have piri piri flavours with chicken, so why can't fish have a turn? This one is pretty hands off, all done on one tray and in under an hour: necessary on busy weeknights!

INGREDIENTS

FOR THE PIRI PIRI SEASONING

2 tbsp smoked paprika

2 tbsp onion granules

2 tbsp garlic granules

1 tbsp salt

1 tbsp granulated sugar

1 tbsp ground coriander

1 tbsp dried oregano

2 tsp dried parsley

1-2 tsp cayenne pepper (depending on how spicy you like it!)

1 tsp ground ginger

FOR THE TRAYBAKE

500g potatoes, cubed

50g breadcrumbs

4 tbsp piri piri sauce (in the heat level of your choice)

4 fillets of salmon

1 lemon, sliced

150g cherry tomatoes, halved

½ red bell pepper, roughly chopped

½ yellow bell pepper, roughly chopped

200g tenderstem broccoli

METHOD

1. First, combine all the ingredients for the piri piri seasoning. Sprinkle half of this over the potatoes with some cooking oil spray and mix until fully coated.

2. Spread the spiced potatoes out on a large baking tray and bake them at 180°c for around 30 minutes, until beginning to brown (or 25 minutes in the air fryer).

3. Meanwhile, mix the other half of the piri piri seasoning with the breadcrumbs. Brush the piri piri sauce over the salmon fillets, then sprinkle the breadcrumbs on top to form a coating.

4. Place the breadcrumbed salmon onto the baking tray between the cooked potatoes and tuck the lemon slices into any gaps, especially around the salmon.

5. Add the cherry tomatoes, chopped bell peppers and tenderstem broccoli to the tray. Spray everything with oil and then bake for another 15 minutes (or 10 minutes in the air fryer).

6. The only addition you could want for this traybake is an extra sauce to dip everything in. I like to make a piri piri yoghurt dip by mixing fat-free Greek yoghurt and piri piri sauce together!

Tips: I like to make my own breadcrumbs using wholemeal bread. If it's not stale, I just toast it first and then blend it into a crumb. It's a great way to use up stale bread though and can be frozen too!

CALS:	CARBS:	FAT:	PROTEIN:	DIETARY:
386	31.5G	15.6G	29.9G	GF (USE GF BREADCRUMBS), DF

French Onion Gnocchi

PREP TIME: 10 MINUTES | COOK TIME: 40 MINUTES | SERVES: 4

Who doesn't love a comforting bowl of French onion soup? This cheat's version turns those classic flavours into an even more comforting bowl of fluffy gnocchi and white beans!

INGREDIENTS

1 tbsp light butter

3 white onions, finely sliced

2 red onions, finely sliced

1 tbsp demerara sugar

50ml balsamic vinegar

6 cloves of garlic, grated

½ tsp dried thyme

400g gnocchi

400g tinned butter beans, drained

1 tbsp Worcestershire Sauce

1 tsp Dijon mustard

250ml beef stock

80g cheddar, grated

METHOD

1. Melt the butter in a pan (ideally an ovenproof one) and then cook the onions on a low heat for around 10 minutes, until they begin to soften. Spray with oil as needed.

2. Stir the sugar and balsamic vinegar into the softened onions and continue to cook for another 15 minutes or so on a low heat.

3. When the onions are soft, jammy, and have a golden colour, push them to the edge of the pan and spray the centre with a little oil.

4. Fry the garlic, thyme, gnocchi, and butter beans in the pan, allowing the gnocchi to crisp up on both sides.

5. Stir in the Worcestershire Sauce, mustard and beef stock. Bring to the boil and then simmer for 10 minutes or so, until the liquid reduces slightly.

6. Once the liquid has reduced to your liking, season the mixture to taste with black pepper, top with the grated cheese and then pop the pan under the grill for about 5 minutes.

7. Once the cheesy top is golden and bubbling, serve the gnocchi straightaway.

Tips: If you want to keep this veggie, you can get beef-flavoured vegetarian stock cubes. I do highly recommend beef stock where possible though! If you can get Gruyre, Gouda, Edam or Comté cheeses to use instead of cheddar, these will add a lovely nutty flavour to the dish.

CALS:	CARBS:	FAT:	PROTEIN:	DIETARY:
432	59G	9.9G	18.3G	VEGGIE (SEE TIP)

Cheesy Broccoli Orzo

PREP TIME: 5 MINUTES | COOK TIME: 20 MINUTES | SERVES: 4

This one is just the most comforting hug in a bowl! Cheddar and broccoli never disappoint, and the orzo soaks up all the delicious flavours, making a super creamy sauce.

INGREDIENTS

2 tsp light butter

1 large white onion, diced

6 cloves of garlic, diced

250g orzo

1 tbsp dried parsley

2 tsp onion granules

1 tsp Dijon mustard

1 tsp wholegrain mustard

750ml stock of your choice

250ml skimmed milk

300g broccoli, roughly chopped into small pieces

150g mature cheddar, grated

METHOD

1. Melt the butter and fry the onion (topped up with up cooking oil spray as needed) until softened, then add the garlic and orzo. Toast for 2 minutes to give the orzo a nutty flavour.

2. Season the orzo with salt and black pepper to taste, then stir in the parsley, onion granules, both mustards, stock, and milk.

3. Bring the liquid to the boil and then simmer on a low heat with a lid on the pan for about 5 minutes.

4. After 5 minutes, remove the lid, add the broccoli and stir well, then return the lid and simmer for another 5 minutes. If the orzo is looking too dry but not yet cooked, add some more stock and/or milk.

5. Once the orzo is cooked, stir in the grated cheese until combined. Serve immediately! I like to eat this as is but if I want to get some extra nutrients in there, I'll have a fresh salad with it.

Tips: A particularly sharp cheddar works well to balance the flavours here. I like making this with chicken stock but use veggie stock to keep it vegetarian friendly if you prefer!

CALS:	CARBS:	FAT:	PROTEIN:	DIETARY:	
313	55.9G	16.1G	22.4G	VEGGIE, GF (USE GF ORZO)	

One Pot Caprese Rice

If you're a fan of the classic flavours of a caprese salad, but fancy something a bit more substantial, this is the dish for you! Minimal ingredients and on the table in under 30 minutes: you can't go wrong.

INGREDIENTS

6 shallots, finely diced
8 cloves of garlic, finely chopped
400g cherry tomatoes
2 tbsp tomato purée
2 tbsp dried oregano
1 tbsp dried basil
50ml balsamic vinegar
200g long grain rice, washed
750ml vegetable stock
250g (2 balls) light mozzarella
2 large tomatoes, sliced

TO SERVE (OPTIONAL)

10g fresh basil
50ml balsamic glaze
Cracked black pepper
Flaky sea salt

METHOD

1. Fry the shallots, garlic and whole cherry tomatoes in an ovenproof pan until the shallots are softened, and the tomatoes are beginning to turn jammy and soft.

2. Add the tomato purée, oregano, basil, and balsamic vinegar to the pan and cook for about 5 minutes, until the tomato begins to caramelise.

3. Add the washed rice, stir to coat the grains in the juices from the pan, then add the stock. Bring to the boil, then cover with a lid and turn the heat down to a simmer.

4. Leave to cook on a low heat for about 15-25 minutes (check on it after 15). You'll know it's done when there is no more liquid, and the rice is almost cooked through.

5. You can add more liquid if your rice seems very underdone after 20 minutes, but only add a little at a time and mix some more tomato purée, basil and oregano into the stock first to keep the flavours of the dish concentrated.

6. Break up one of the balls of mozzarella and stir it through the rice until melted. Slice up the remaining mozzarella ball and lay this on top along with the sliced tomatoes.

7. Grill the dish until golden and bubbly on top. I like to garnish it with fresh basil, a drizzle of balsamic glaze, some cracked black pepper, and flaky sea salt just before serving.

Tips: It's worth getting the best quality tomatoes here – I like them on the vine! You can also get tinned cherry tomatoes, which are a great alternative. To keep this veggie-friendly, use a vegetable stock but make sure it's a good quality one. You can sometimes get tomato-flavoured stock which would be even better! If you don't mind about keeping it veggie, you can use chicken stock.

CALS:	CARBS:	FAT:	PROTEIN:	DIETARY:
318	27G	13.8G	19.9G	VEGGIE, GF

Creamy Harissa Hake

PREP TIME: 5 MINUTES | COOK TIME: 30 MINUTES | SERVES: 4

If you're looking for a new way to serve fish, this one is for you! The creaminess of the sauce perfectly balances out the spice from the harissa and you can have it on the table in 30 minutes.

INGREDIENTS

4 fillets of hake

4 shallots, finely diced

4 cloves of garlic, finely diced

100g roasted red pepper in brine, drained and chopped

2 tbsp harissa paste

2 tbsp tomato purée

½ lemon, juiced

300ml stock of your choice

1 tbsp cornflour, mixed with cold water

75g light cream cheese

100g kale

METHOD

1. Season the hake with salt and black pepper and then fry in some cooking oil spray until lightly golden on each side. Remove from the pan and set aside.

2. Using the same pan, fry the shallots, garlic and roasted red pepper until the onion begins to soften.

3. Stir in the harissa paste, tomato purée, lemon juice, and stock. Allow this to simmer and reduce a little before adding the cornflour paste and stirring until thickened.

4. Once the sauce has thickened, add the cream cheese and stir until combined, then sit the hake fillets in the pan and scatter over the kale.

5. Pop the lid on the pan and allow everything to simmer until the hake is cooked through and the kale has wilted.

6. Season to taste with salt and black pepper as needed, then serve immediately. I love this with air fried crispy potatoes and either a lemony salad, or tenderstem broccoli cooked in a griddle pan with lemon juice.

Tips: Any greens will work here instead of kale: try cavolo nero, broccoli, spinach, spring greens, or whatever you fancy! I think chicken stock works well in this recipe, but you can also use veg or fish stock if you like. This is great with other firm fish like salmon or cod too!

CALS:	CARBS:	FAT:	PROTEIN:	DIETARY:
198	10.2G	4.6G	31.2G	GF

WHIP IT UP WEDNESDAYS

Hooray, we're halfway through the week! Wednesdays can be busy, and when you're right in the thick of it, the last thing you want to do is spend hours cooking. These recipes are all about keeping it minimalistic with fewer ingredients, quicker cooking times, simpler cooking methods and less to wash up: just keeping it simple but always getting a healthy, hearty meal on the table.

Mexican Cod

PREP TIME: 5 MINUTES | COOK TIME: 20 MINUTES | SERVES: 4

The key to this recipe is fresh, good quality ingredients: there aren't many, and it doesn't take long to cook, so each ingredient plays an important role! Luckily, everything you need is budget-friendly and easy to get hold of.

INGREDIENTS

4 x 125g pieces of cod (approx. 500g total)

300g large tomatoes, roughly chopped

2 red onions, roughly chopped

1 red bell pepper, roughly chopped

1 yellow bell pepper, roughly chopped

6 cloves of garlic, roughly chopped

1-2 jalapeños, sliced (optional – deseed if you want to reduce the heat level)

1 tbsp smoked paprika

2 tsp ground cumin

1 tsp chilli powder

1 lime, juiced

10g chopped fresh coriander, plus extra to serve if you like

METHOD

1. Season the cod with salt and pepper. Fry in a pan with some cooking oil spray until golden on both sides and almost cooked through, then transfer to a plate.

2. Now add the tomatoes, onions, bell peppers, garlic, and jalapeños (if using) to the pan and cook until softened.

3. Season the tomato mixture with the smoked paprika, cumin, chilli powder, salt and pepper. Stir in the lime juice and fresh coriander, then add the fish back to the pan.

4. Cook with a lid on for around 5 minutes, until the cod is fully cooked through. I like to serve this with even more fresh coriander on top, alongside rice and corn on the cob!

Tips: Any firm white fish will work for this recipe, such as (unsmoked) haddock or hake. Add the jalapeños if you like a kick but feel free to skip them if not! I like to use fresh ones where possible, rather than the ones in brine. You can also use other green chillies if you can't get jalapeños.

CALS:	CARBS:	FAT:	PROTEIN:	DIETARY:
130	25.3G	0.3G	21.2G	GF, DF

Creamy Peppercorn Chicken Pasta

PREP TIME: 5 MINUTES | COOK TIME: 25 MINUTES | SERVES: 4

Steak and peppercorn sauce always feels like such a treat; here the flavours are still indulgent, but in a more accessible 'everyday' weeknight dinner made with staple ingredients.

INGREDIENTS

400g chicken breast, sliced

1 tsp salt

2 tsp smoked paprika

Freshly ground black pepper, to taste

300g chestnut mushrooms, roughly chopped

2 tbsp black peppercorns, roughly crushed

2 tsp light butter

1 white onion, finely diced

6 cloves of garlic, grated

200g pasta of your choice

250ml beef stock

75g light cream cheese

Handful of fresh parsley (optional)

METHOD

1. Season the sliced chicken with the salt, smoked paprika and lots of black pepper. In a large pan, fry it with some cooking oil spray until all sides have some colour.

2. Add the mushrooms and peppercorns to the pan and continue to cook until the mushrooms are browned on all sides.

3. Add the butter, onion and garlic to the pan. Cook on a low heat until the onion is softened and beginning to brown, topping up with cooking oil spray if the mixture becomes too dry.

4. Meanwhile, cook your pasta according to the package instructions (although I like to add a beef stock cube to the cooking water instead of salt here).

5. Add the stock to the chicken mixture, bring to the boil and keep the pan on a high heat until the liquid reduces.

6. Finish the sauce by stirring in the cream cheese, then adjust the seasoning to taste (I always want more black pepper!).

7. Using a slotted spoon, transfer the cooked pasta straight into the sauce along with some of the cooking water and give it a good stir to emulsify everything.

8. This is lovely served with some fresh parsley and a sprinkle of smoked paprika on top. It also goes well with crispy garlic bread to soak up all that lovely sauce, and a side salad to cut through the rich flavours.

Tips: I do think beef stock works best here, but feel free to use chicken, veg, or even a mushroom stock cube if you can get it. If you have mushroom haters in your house, just skip the mushrooms!

CALS:	CARBS:	FAT:	PROTEIN:	
359	39G	6.05G	39.9G	

Sweet Chilli Chicken Bakes

PREP TIME: 10 MINUTES | COOK TIME: 15 MINUTES | SERVES: 4

Using tortilla wraps is a great hack to replicate pastry and this is an easy way to make hot bakes or pasties like you can get in a bakery. The sweet chilli chicken filling is a guaranteed crowd pleaser!

INGREDIENTS

400g chicken breast, diced into small pieces

1 yellow bell pepper, diced

1 red bell pepper, diced

1 tbsp smoked paprika

2 tsp garlic granules

1 tsp onion granules

1 tsp chilli powder

½ tsp salt

½ tsp black pepper

40g cheddar, grated

40g mozzarella, grated

100g light cream cheese

75ml sweet chilli sauce

4 tortilla wraps, halved

1 egg, beaten

METHOD

1. Fry the chicken and bell pepper with the smoked paprika, garlic and onion granules, chilli powder, salt, and black pepper in some cooking oil spray.

2. Once cooked through, transfer the chicken mixture to a bowl. Add the grated cheeses, cream cheese and sweet chilli sauce, then mix everything together well.

3. Lay out the halved tortilla wraps and divide the filling evenly between them, placing it on one side of each half and leaving a border around the edge of the wrap.

4. Brush the edges of the wraps with the beaten egg, then fold the empty side over the filling and press down with your fingers to enclose it. Press the edges with a fork to fully seal them.

5. Place the parcels on a baking tray lined with greaseproof paper and then brush the tops with beaten egg to glaze them.

6. Oven bake for 10 minutes at 180°c or air fry for 8 minutes at 180°c until the wraps are golden and crispy on the outside.

7. These quick bakes are great for a snack or lunch – and they freeze well too – but for a more substantial meal, I like them with air fried chips and peas or greens.

Tips: If you're feeling extra lazy, you can just wrap whole tortillas around the filling like a burrito, then spray with oil and cook in the same way instead of making parcels – you'll get a very similar result!

CALS:	CARBS:	FAT:	PROTEIN:
403	34G	17.8G	43.4G

Char Siu Chicken Rolls

PREP TIME: 15 MINUTES | COOK TIME: 15 MINUTES | SERVES: 4

Char siu is Chinese cuisine's answer to BBQ sauce; it's more fragrant and usually served with pork, but it goes perfectly with the chicken here!

INGREDIENTS

500g chicken mince

1 tsp Chinese five spice

1 tsp white pepper

1 tsp sesame oil

1 tbsp honey

2 tbsp hoisin sauce

2 tbsp dark soy sauce

6 cloves of garlic, grated

1 thumb-sized piece of ginger, grated

3 spring onions, finely chopped

4 tortilla wraps

1 egg, beaten

2 tsp sesame seeds

METHOD

1. Mix the chicken mince with the Chinese five spice, white pepper, sesame oil, honey, hoisin sauce, soy sauce, garlic, ginger, and spring onion.

2. Divide the mixture into 4 equal portions. Lay out the tortilla wraps and spoon a portion onto each one, forming the mince mixture into a sausage shape down the middle of the wrap.

3. Brush the edges of the tortilla wraps with the beaten egg and then roll up to enclose the filling. Cut each one in half so you have 8 rolls.

4. Place the rolls on a baking tray lined with greaseproof paper, making sure the seam where the wrap was rolled up is underneath. Egg wash the tops of the rolls, then sprinkle with the sesame seeds which should stick to the egg.

5. Bake the rolls in the oven at 180°c for around 15-20 minutes, until the tops are golden and the filling is cooked through. You can also air fry these for 10 minutes at 180°c.

6. I like to serve mine with greens fried in a teaspoon of sesame oil and finished off with some soy sauce, and chips are always good too!

Tips: If you want to check the seasoning in your mince mixture before you commit to cooking them all, just take a tiny bit and fry it in a pan until it's cooked. Taste and adjust the seasonings as needed. I like to use a mixture of black and white sesame seeds, but either is fine. These rolls also make a great snack or lunch option.

CALS:	CARBS:	FAT:	PROTEIN:	DIETARY:		
379	42.5G	8.5G	31.1G	GF (USE GF WRAPS), DF		

Bacon & Egg Fried Rice

PREP TIME: 5 MINUTES | COOK TIME: 10 MINUTES | SERVES: 4

This recipe is super satisfying, thanks to a small handful of basic ingredients that make a delicious meal in no time at all. Although you might not expect it, it's also a great recipe for boosting your veg intake thanks to the cauliflower rice!

INGREDIENTS

8 rashers of smoked streaky bacon

1 thumb-sized piece of ginger, grated

4 cloves of garlic, grated

300g short grain white rice, cooked and cooled

4 tbsp dark soy sauce

2 tbsp light soy sauce

2 tsp onion granules

1 tsp Chinese five spice

4 eggs, beaten

150g cauliflower rice

White pepper, to taste

Spring onions (optional)

METHOD

1. Lay the bacon rashers in a cold pan and place over a medium heat. Fry until the bacon begins to brown and become crispy.

2. Add the ginger and garlic to the pan along with some cooking oil spray if needed. Stir fry until fragrant, then add the cooked white rice and break it up so the flavours are mixed through.

3. Once the rice is starting to warm through, add the soy sauces, onion granules and Chinese five spice.

4. Mix everything together well, then push the rice to the edges of the pan to make space in the middle. Pour the beaten eggs into this space and leave for 30 seconds or so to let them set on the bottom of the pan, then scramble without mixing them into the rice yet.

5. Once the egg is no longer liquid, stir it through the rice and add the cauliflower rice. Allow it all to heat through and mix until everything is combined.

6. Season the fried rice to taste with white pepper and salt if you feel it needs it (soy sauce usually adds enough saltiness for me!).

7. Serve immediately, with some finely sliced spring onion on top for garnish if you like.

Tips: If you use sesame oil when cooking the ginger and garlic, you'll get more of an authentic Asian flavour in the fried rice. I never buy cauliflower rice as it tastes so much better and is so easy to make at home; it's just grated cauliflower! I don't recommend using a blender to make cauliflower rice, as the pieces end up too small and it doesn't taste as good. You can cheat and use microwaveable packets of rice if you forget to cook some before-hand. Alternatively, this recipe is a great way to use up leftover rice! To make this in the air fryer, cook the bacon for 3-4 minutes at 180°c and then add the ginger, garlic, rice, soy sauces, onion granules, and Chinese five spice. Mix well, then cook for 5 minutes at 200°c. Finally, mix in the cauliflower rice, make a well in the middle, add the egg and cook for 3-4 minutes at 180°c until set. Mix everything together and serve.

CALS:	CARBS:	FAT:	PROTEIN:	DIETARY:
481	68.7G	15.5G	21.1G	DF

Chorizo Carbonara

PREP TIME: 5 MINUTES | COOK TIME: 10 MINUTES | SERVES: 4

Swapping the bacon for chorizo in this carbonara is a small but mighty change that brings in a lovely smoky flavour. You'll likely have most of these ingredients in already and it's done in 15 minutes!

INGREDIENTS

240g pasta of your choice (I recommend linguine or spaghetti)

6 egg yolks

100g parmesan, grated

100g chorizo, diced

1 lemon, zested and juiced

Chopped fresh parsley, to taste (optional)

METHOD

1. First, put your pasta on to boil in a large pan of heavily salted water. Whisk the egg yolks and parmesan together in a small bowl and set aside.

2. Fry the chorizo in a large pan until some of the oils are released. Once the pasta is al dente, transfer it straight from the water to the pan and toss to coat in all the chorizo juices.

3. Take the pan off the heat and pour in the egg and parmesan mixture. Quickly mix it through, using tongs or tossing everything together, until your sauce becomes glossy. Add small spoonfuls of pasta water as needed to help everything come together.

4. Finish the carbonara by mixing in the zest and juice of the lemon, and the chopped fresh parsley if using.

5. I like mine served with a side salad dressed with balsamic vinegar, and some garlic bread of course. Don't forget to finish it with lots of black pepper and extra parsley on top!

Tips: The key to carbonara is to just keep stirring: the more you stir, the more you are going to release the starches from the pasta which helps to create that glossy sauce and stops the egg from scrambling.

CALS:	CARBS:	FAT:	PROTEIN:
476	44.8G	21.2G	24.6G

Maple Mustard Glazed Pork

PREP TIME: 5 MINUTES | COOK TIME: 15 MINUTES | SERVES: 4

I always make this one when autumn comes around; it's so cosy, especially when served with mashed potatoes! With a quick cooking time and only six ingredients, it's one I come back to again and again on busy weeknights.

INGREDIENTS

4 pork loin medallions, trimmed of all fat

2 tsp smoked paprika

2 tsp garlic granules

1 tsp onion granules

4 tbsp maple syrup

1 tbsp wholegrain mustard

METHOD

1. Coat the pork loins with the smoked paprika, garlic and onion granules, and salt and pepper to taste.

2. Fry in a pan with some cooking oil spray until browned on both sides and almost cooked through, which should take about 10 minutes.

3. Mix the maple syrup and mustard together, then brush this onto the pork in the pan. Keep glazing and flipping the pork until you run out of the glaze, and everything is golden and sticky.

4. This glazed pork is delicious served with mash (either white or sweet potatoes work well) and it's also great with roasted root veg like pumpkin, squash and parsnips. Of course, you need some greens on the side too! Enjoy it with peas, broccoli, cabbage, or green beans.

Tips: This recipe also works well with chicken breasts or thighs. You can cook this in the air fryer too! It will need 9 minutes at 190°c, making sure you flip and baste the pork halfway through.

CALS:	CARBS:	FAT:	PROTEIN:	DIETARY:
183	11.6G	4.9G	23.2G	GF (CHECK THE MUSTARD), DF

Pesto Parma Ham Cod

PREP TIME: 5 MINUTES | COOK TIME: 10 MINUTES | SERVES: 4

With just five ingredients, all done in one tray, and taking just 15 minutes in total, this recipe has saved me many times on a busy weeknight!

INGREDIENTS

8 slices of Parma ham
4 x 125g pieces of cod (approx. 500g total)
1 lemon, juiced
300g cherry tomatoes
1 heaped tbsp light pesto

METHOD

1. Lay 2 slices of Parma ham on top of each other in opposite directions to form a cross.

2. Place a piece of cod in the middle of the cross, splash on a bit of lemon juice, season with a bit of black pepper, then fold the Parma ham over the cod to make a parcel.

3. Repeat this with all your cod and Parma ham to make 4 parcels, then place these on a baking tray with the seam (where you wrapped the ham around the cod) underneath.

4. Mix the cherry tomatoes with the pesto and put these in the baking tray with the parcels.

5. Bake in the oven at 180°c for about 10 minutes (depending on the thickness of your fish). You can also air fry this at 180°c for about 8 minutes.

6. My favourite way to serve this is with crispy potatoes coated in oregano, salt and black pepper (usually I do these in the air fryer) alongside some salad or greens!

Tips: You can season the tomatoes with salt too if you like, but I find that their acidity balances out the saltiness of the Parma ham perfectly.

CALS:	CARBS:	FAT:	PROTEIN:	DIETARY:
225	4.3G	6.85G	34.3G	GF, DF (CHECK THE PESTO)

Sticky Ginger Seabass

PREP TIME: 10 MINUTES | COOK TIME: 15 MINUTES | SERVES: 2

I love a simple meal like this: minimal ingredients, minimal fuss, but maximum flavour!

INGREDIENTS

3 tbsp dark soy sauce

3 tbsp light soy sauce

1 lemon, zested

1 thumb-sized piece of ginger, grated

3 cloves of garlic, grated

2 tbsp honey

2 fillets of seabass (approx. 180g total)

200g pak choi, halved

TO SERVE (OPTIONAL)

Fresh coriander

Fresh ginger

Fresh chilli

METHOD

1. Mix the dark soy sauce, light soy sauce, lemon zest, ginger, garlic, and honey together. Slice the zested lemon and set aside.

2. Spray a pan with some oil and then add the seabass, skin side down, and the pak choi, cut side down. Fry until the pak choi chars on the edges and the seabass is becoming firmer.

3. Flip the seabass and pak choi over, throw in the lemon slices, and pour in the sauce you made earlier.

4. Turn the heat up high and cook until the sauce is sticky, ensuring the seabass and pak choi are cooked through. Flip them once more so they are fully coated in the sauce.

5. This goes perfectly with some sticky rice or jasmine rice, and I like to serve it with fresh coriander leaves and slices of fresh ginger and chilli on top.

Tips: You can make this with any white fish such as cod, hake or haddock. It works with chicken and pork too! Use sesame oil instead of cooking oil spray for an extra punch of flavour.

CALS:	CARBS:	FAT:	PROTEIN:	DIETARY:
294	25.2G	9.25G	27.2G	GF, DF

Pesto Spinach Fritters

PREP TIME: 10 MINUTES | COOK TIME: 10 MINUTES | SERVES: 4

These budget friendly fritters have the added bonus of just 20 minutes cooking time and only seven ingredients – exactly what you want to hear on a weeknight!

INGREDIENTS

350g fresh spinach
350g ricotta
4 cloves of garlic, finely grated
1 egg, beaten
75g plain flour
50g pecorino, grated
3 tbsp light pesto

METHOD

1. Wilt the spinach in a dry pan, then let it cool before squeezing out any excess water.

2. Mix the prepared spinach with the ricotta, grated garlic, egg, flour, pecorino, and pesto, then season the mixture to taste with salt and black pepper.

3. Shape the spinach mixture into 8 patties, spray a frying pan with oil and fry them for 3-4 minutes on each side over a low-medium heat, until the outside begins to brown and the inside warms through.

4. Alternatively, you can cook the fritters in the air fryer for 8-10 minutes at 180°c.

5. I like to serve these fritters with a marinara-style sauce, which I usually make a cheat's version of by mixing passata or chopped tomatoes with Italian herbs, balsamic vinegar, salt, and pepper. They also go well with crispy air fried or roasted potatoes.

Tips: This mixture is also lovely made into 'meatballs' and again they go well with the tomato sauce! If you want these fritters to be 100% vegetarian, make sure you pick a suitable hard cheese as parmesan, pecorino and Grana Padano are not always vegetarian.

CALS:	CARBS:	FAT:	PROTEIN:	DIETARY:
267	17.6G	13.9G	17.1G	VEGGIE (SEE TIPS)

THROW IT IN THURSDAYS

Thursday might be the day you end up having to do the dreaded 'top up shop' yet still have lots of odds and ends in the fridge that you want to use up before the weekend shop. These recipes will help you use up every bit of food in your fridge and cupboards, reducing waste and saving you money!

Chicken & Broccoli Stem Stir Fry

PREP TIME: 10 MINUTES | COOK TIME: 15 MINUTES | SERVES: 4

It always annoys me that so much of a head of broccoli seems to go to waste. That doesn't have to be the case with this quick and easy stir fry in an addictive garlicky sauce!

INGREDIENTS

400g chicken breast, sliced

½ tsp bicarbonate of soda

1 tbsp cornflour

4 tbsp light soy sauce

1 head of broccoli, stem only

300ml chicken stock

2 tbsp honey

2 tbsp dark soy sauce

1 tbsp rice vinegar

8 cloves of garlic, roughly chopped

1 tsp fresh ginger, grated

½ tsp Chinese five spice

½ tsp white pepper

1 red bell pepper, roughly chopped

1 green bell pepper, roughly chopped

6 spring onions, finely chopped (whites and greens separated)

METHOD

1. Add the sliced chicken to a bowl with the bicarbonate of soda, cornflour and 2 tablespoons of the light soy sauce. Mix thoroughly and then leave to sit for a minimum of 10 minutes while you prepare your other ingredients.

2. Peel the broccoli stem just until you get to a greener, slightly softer centre. Slice this into rounds.

3. Make your stir fry sauce for later by combining the chicken stock, honey, remaining light soy sauce, dark soy sauce, rice vinegar, garlic, ginger, Chinese five spice, and white pepper.

4. First, fry the marinated chicken until cooked through which should only take a few minutes, then remove from the pan and set aside.

5. Using the same pan, add the broccoli stem and bell pepper but just leave them to sit until they become slightly charred around the edges.

6. Now you can stir, and add the whites of the spring onions. Once these soften slightly, pour in the sauce and turn the heat up.

7. Allow the sauce to bubble and thicken (stir in 1 tablespoon of cornflour mixed to a paste with cold water here if you prefer a thicker sauce).

8. Finally, add the chicken back to the pan and give everything a good stir to coat your stir fry in the sauce.

9. Serve immediately with the spring onion greens on top and either boiled or fried rice on the side. I also love to bake or air fry some kale coated in salt, sweetener and Chinese five spice as it tastes just like crispy seaweed from a takeaway!

Tips: Substitute the rice vinegar for white wine vinegar, lemon juice or lime juice if you don't have any. You can of course add other vegetables to this – use up what you have! I also particularly love bamboo shoots and water chestnuts in a stir fry. Sesame oil will add another layer of flavour to your stir fry if you have some in the cupboard.

CALS:	CARBS:	FAT:	PROTEIN:	DIETARY:
218	12.6G	2.1G	36.3G	DF

Chicken & Apple Chilli Jam Meatballs

PREP TIME: 10 MINUTES | COOK TIME: 15 MINUTES | SERVES: 4

The perfect way to use up the apples that have been to work or school and back every day in everyone's lunchboxes; they are put to much better use in this sweet and spicy recipe!

INGREDIENTS

600g chicken mince

1 apple, peeled and grated

2 tsp smoked paprika

2 tsp garlic granules

1 tsp onion granules

1 tsp chilli powder

1 tsp salt

½ tsp white pepper

200g chilli jam

TO SERVE (OPTIONAL)

Spring onions

Sesame seeds

METHOD

1. Mix the chicken mince with the grated apple, smoked paprika, garlic and onion granules, chilli powder, salt, and white pepper until fully combined.

2. Roll the chicken mix into 16-20 meatballs weighing 25-30g each. Pan fry or air fry the meatballs until they're golden on all sides and cooked through (10 minutes at 180°c in the air fryer should do this).

3. Add the chilli jam to a pan on a high heat and let it get sticky, then add the meatballs and stir to coat in the glaze.

4. Serve immediately topped with sliced spring onions and sesame seeds if you like. These go well with rice or noodles, or just a salad if you want to keep it light!

Tips: You need to serve these immediately, or the chilli jam will cool down and become impossibly sticky!
If freezing, I would recommend just cooking and freezing the meatballs, then making the chilli jam part fresh when you want to serve them, as it only takes a few minutes!

CALS:	CARBS:	FAT:	PROTEIN:	DIETARY:
254	31.8G	2.8G	23.7G	GF, DF

Potato Nachos

PREP TIME: 10 MINUTES | COOK TIME: 40 MINUTES | SERVES: 4

Potato slices are a great base to use for nachos; they're sturdier than tortilla chips, contain more fibre, and it's just a great way to use up all those wonky potatoes that you don't quite know what to do with!

INGREDIENTS

750g potatoes (Maris Pipers work well)
1 tbsp smoked paprika
1 tbsp dried oregano
2 tsp garlic granules
2 tsp onion granules
1 tsp salt
1 tsp black pepper
50g cheddar, grated
50g mozzarella, grated

FOR THE BBQ CHICKEN TOPPING

3 chicken breasts
2 tbsp BBQ seasoning
4 tbsp BBQ sauce

METHOD

1. Chop your potatoes into 'tortilla chips' – you can literally just slice them into rounds, but if I really want them to look authentic, I'll chop the potatoes into slices lengthways and then chop those slices into rough triangles (with some rounded edges of course!).

2. Next, make your spice mix. Combine the smoked paprika, oregano, garlic and onion granules, salt, and black pepper in a small bowl.

3. Spray the sliced potatoes with oil and then sprinkle over the spice mix. Give them a good mix to make sure they're all coated, then arrange on one or more baking trays in a single layer.

4. Oven bake the potatoes at 170°c for 20 minutes, give them a shake, turn up the oven to 200°c and cook for another 15 minutes.

5. You can also air fry the potatoes at 190°c for about 25 minutes, just give them a shake halfway through and make sure your air fryer isn't too overcrowded (they can be in a few layers for this though).

6. Meanwhile, make your toppings. I like to coat chicken breasts with BBQ seasoning, then oven bake or air fry for 20-25 minutes before shredding and mixing the meat with BBQ sauce.

7. Collect all your 'tortilla chips' together in a pile on a baking tray or in a baking dish, add your topping and the grated cheeses, then bake for another 5-10 minutes.

8. Once everything is heated through and the cheese has melted, finish the nachos with any of your other favourite toppings. You could add salsa, guacamole, sour cream (I like fat-free Greek yoghurt as a substitute), jalapeños, chives, spring onions, and more!

Tips: You can top your nachos with whatever you like – chicken, veggie chilli, pulled pork – but my favourite is BBQ pulled chicken!

CALS:	CARBS:	FAT:	PROTEIN:	DIETARY:
373	35.7G	8.8G	32.6G	GF

Potato Skin Tacos

PREP TIME: 15 MINUTES | COOK TIME: 25 MINUTES | SERVES: 4

No taco shells? No problem! Make crispy taco shells – perfect for scooping up lots of that delicious filling – with potato skins! This is a great way to add fibre to your taco night and reduce waste too.

INGREDIENTS

4 large potatoes (Maris Pipers work well)

4 tsp smoked paprika

2 tsp black pepper

1 tsp salt

1 white onion, diced

6 cloves of garlic, crushed

500g lean beef mince

50g tomato purée

1 beef stock cube

2 tsp dried oregano

1 tsp ground cumin

1 tsp dried coriander leaf

½ tsp ground coriander

½ tsp chilli powder

METHOD

1. Microwave your potatoes until soft in the middle (about 10-15 minutes, flipping them over halfway through) and then slice them in half. Carefully scoop out the insides, saving them for another meal (see the tips below for some ideas).

2. Spray the potato skins on both sides with oil, then sprinkle over half the smoked paprika and black pepper along with the salt.

3. Oven bake them at 180°c for about 15 minutes or air fry for 10 minutes, until the skins have crisped up.

4. Meanwhile, make the taco filling. Fry the onion and garlic in cooking oil spray until softened. Add the beef mince, tomato purée, beef stock cube, oregano, cumin, dried coriander leaf, ground coriander, chilli powder, and the remaining smoked paprika and black pepper.

5. Fry the spiced beef mixture until the mince has browned. If it looks dry, add a splash of boiling water to loosen it up.

6. Serve the beef filling inside your potato skin taco shells, then finish with your favourite toppings! I like grated cheese (spicy cheese if I can find it), fresh coriander, guacamole, salsa, and sour cream (or fat-free Greek yoghurt!).

Tips: The leftover potato insides are great for turning into mashed potatoes or adding to fishcakes. I like to serve these tacos with some spicy rice and salad on the side for a more substantial meal!

CALS:	CARBS:	FAT:	PROTEIN:	DIETARY:
299	31.9G	5.8G	30G	GF (CHECK THE STOCK CUBE) DF

Ham & Cheese Hasselback Potato Bake

PREP TIME: 10 MINUTES | COOK TIME: 55 MINUTES | SERVES: 4

This is my favourite way to use up those annoying potatoes that get left in the bottom of the bag… you know the ones: they're too annoying to peel for mash, and too small to cut into chips, so you end up throwing them away. Not anymore!

INGREDIENTS

750g small-medium potatoes

3 tsp onion granules

3 tsp garlic granules

300ml skimmed milk

1 tbsp cornflour, mixed with cold water

150g cheddar, finely grated

1 tsp wholegrain mustard

200g ham slices

Fresh parsley and chives, to serve (optional)

METHOD

1. Put a pair of chopsticks, skewers or wooden spoons either side of a potato, and cut slices all along to create a hasselback pattern (you only need 4-5 cuts in each potato). Repeat this with all the potatoes. You'll get faster at this the more you do, I promise!

2. Spray the hasselback potatoes with oil and season with salt, black pepper, 2 teaspoons of the onion granules and 1 teaspoon of the garlic granules.

3. Bake the potatoes in the oven at 200°c for about 35 minutes until they are very nearly done.

4. Meanwhile, make the cheesy sauce. Gently warm the milk, then add the cornflour paste and stir until thickened. Finish with half the grated cheddar along with the mustard, remaining onion and garlic granules, and some black pepper. Pour the sauce into an ovenproof dish.

5. Remove the potatoes from the oven and add slices of ham to the slits in the potatoes (it doesn't have to be every single one).

6. Sit the potatoes in the cheese sauce and sprinkle over the remaining cheddar. Bake for 15-20 minutes, until the sauce is bubbling and the potatoes are fully cooked with golden tops.

7. This is lovely served with a refreshing salad dressed with lemon juice or a fat-free French vinaigrette. I also like to sprinkle fresh chives and parsley on top of the bake to serve!

Tips: You can use any potatoes for this, just try to make sure they're all a similar size so that everything can cook evenly. You can make one large bake or use smaller casserole dishes to make individual portions.

CALS:	CARBS:	FAT:	PROTEIN:	DIETARY:
397	36.6G	14.5G	28.6G	GF

Tuna Melt Fishcakes

PREP TIME: 30 MINUTES | COOK TIME: 10 MINUTES | SERVES: 4

If you enjoy a tuna melt, these are for you! The crispy cheese and onion coating pairs perfectly with the cheesy tuna centre. A great way to use up potatoes, spring onions, and cupboard staples.

INGREDIENTS

3 medium potatoes

3 eggs

3 tins of tuna, drained

2 tbsp fat-free Greek yoghurt

8 spring onions, finely sliced

100g cheddar (from a block)

4 packets of cheese and onion crisps

METHOD

1. Microwave your potatoes until soft in the middle (about 10 minutes, flipping them over halfway through) and then slice them in half. Carefully scoop out the insides, saving the skins for another meal (why not try the potato skin tacos on page 92?).

2. In a bowl combine the potato with one of the eggs, the drained tuna, Greek yoghurt, and spring onions, plus salt and pepper to taste.

3. Chop the cheddar into 8 chunks, then wrap an eighth of the tuna mixture around each chunk of cheese, shaping them into flat fishcakes.

4. Pop these in the fridge for a minimum of 20 minutes to help them firm up, which makes the next step easier. Sometimes I do this the night before I want to cook them, if I remember and have time!

5. Beat the remaining 2 eggs and crush the crisps (you can just do this in the bag or use a blender if you don't mind the extra washing up!), placing them into separate shallow bowls.

6. Carefully dip the chilled fishcakes into the beaten egg, letting the excess drip off, then dip into the crisps to form a crunchy coating.

7. Place the fishcakes on a baking tray, spray with oil and then bake at 180°c for 10-15 minutes (or air fry at 170°c for 10 minutes) until the coating is crispy and the cheesy centre has melted.

8. I like to serve these with a simple salad, or a pile of greens like broccoli and peas. They're a great lunch option too (only if you're working from home though — no one wants fish in the office!).

Tips: Although I've used tuna here, you can use most fish in this recipe, tinned or not, as long as it flakes! Mackerel, salmon, cod, or haddock all work well. Rather than using fresh potatoes, you can also use leftover mashed potatoes, or even instant mashed potatoes! You'll need about 400-500g if so. You can use any flavour crisps for the coating, but cheese and onion work really well here! Just make sure they're potato crisps, not maize-based as those types of crisps disintegrate in the egg instead of forming a crispy coating.

CALS:	CARBS:	FAT:	PROTEIN:	DIETARY:
489	23.8G	20.6G	37.4G	GF

Cheesy Leek Hake Bake

PREP TIME: 10 MINUTES | COOK TIME: 25 MINUTES | SERVES: 4

If you're looking for something a bit different to do with your plain white fish, serving it with cheesy leeks is the way to go!

INGREDIENTS

4 fillets of hake
2 tsp dried oregano
2 leeks, washed and sliced
1 tbsp light butter
200ml skimmed milk
1 tbsp cornflour, mixed with cold water
75g parmesan, grated
2 tsp garlic granules
2 tsp dried parsley
1 tsp dried thyme
75g mozzarella, grated

METHOD

1. Season the fish fillets with oregano, salt and pepper. Pan fry or air fry the hake until it is cooked through (8-10 minutes at 180°c in the air fryer should be enough, depending on the thickness of your fish) and then place it in an ovenproof dish.

2. Meanwhile, fry the leeks in the light butter and a little cooking oil spray until softened and beginning to brown. Make sure you cook a lot of moisture out of them at this stage.

3. Add the milk to the leeks and allow to warm through gently, then stir in the cornflour paste and mix well until combined.

4. Once the sauce is beginning to thicken, stir in 50g of the parmesan along with the garlic granules, parsley and thyme. Season to taste with salt and pepper if you like.

5. Pour the sauce over the fish in the ovenproof dish, then top with the grated mozzarella and remaining parmesan.

6. Pop the dish under the grill for 5 minutes or so, until the cheese on top is golden and bubbling. This is best served with either mashed potatoes or crispy herby potatoes alongside steamed tenderstem broccoli and asparagus.

Tips: Any white fish like hake or haddock, or even salmon, will work well in this recipe.

CALS:	CARBS:	FAT:	PROTEIN:	DIETARY:
329	9G	16.6G	34.1G	GF

Creamy Mac & Cheese

PREP TIME: 30 MINUTES | COOK TIME: 20 MINUTES | SERVES: 4

This mac and cheese tastes extra indulgent and creamy, all thanks to a secret ingredient… It's a great way to reduce waste, and perhaps sneak in some veggies for any fussy eaters in the house!

INGREDIENTS

1 butternut squash (approx. 800g)
1 large white onion, finely diced
6 cloves of garlic, finely chopped
300ml skimmed milk
1 tsp Dijon mustard
1-2 tsp wholegrain mustard
1 tbsp cornflour
40g cheddar, grated
40g parmesan, grated
240g pasta of your choice (I recommend spirali or macaroni)

TO SERVE (OPTIONAL)

30g parmesan, grated
30g cheddar, grated
1 packet of crisps

METHOD

1. First, prepare your butternut squash purée. Chop the butternut squash into roughly 4cm cubes, spray with oil, then roast in the oven for 30-40 minutes at 180°c until softened.

2. Separate the flesh from the skin and mash the flesh or use a blender to purée it. This will make more purée than you need but the rest can be frozen for another time!

3. Fry the onion and garlic with some cooking oil spray on a medium-low heat until softened. Stir in the milk and mustards along with salt and pepper to taste, then let this warm through.

4. Mix the cornflour with 1 tablespoon of cold water to make a smooth paste, then add this to your sauce and stir continuously until it thickens slightly.

5. Finally, add the grated cheeses and 250g of the butternut squash purée from earlier. Mix well and leave this to simmer on a low heat.

6. Meanwhile, cook your pasta according to the instructions on the packet. I like to boil mine in stock for extra flavour!

7. Once the pasta is cooked, drain it (saving a mugful of the water) and then stir into the sauce. If the sauce is too thick and not coating the pasta well, add a splash of the cooking water and stir continuously until you have the right consistency.

8. Now you can stop here and eat it like this – which is delicious – or you can take it to the next level and bake it!

9. If you're baking the mac and cheese, transfer it to a large ovenproof dish and then sprinkle over the extra grated parmesan and cheddar. I like to add a crunched-up packet of crisps too; I know it sounds odd but trust me!

10. Bake the mac and cheese for around 10 minutes at 200°c until bubbling and golden on top.

Tips: You can also use frozen pre-prepared butternut squash for this recipe! You can use the remaining butternut squash purée for more mac and cheese of course, but it's also great for stirring into soups and other sauces to sweeten, thicken and add a creamy texture to them. Skip the parmesan or find a vegetarian hard Italian cheese if you want to keep this 100% veggie. You can use any crisps for the topping, but I think smoky bacon or cheese and onion flavour are extra delicious here.

CALS:	CARBS:	FAT:	PROTEIN:	DIETARY:
455	27G	13.75G	18.3G	VEGGIE

Spinach & Feta Slices

PREP TIME: 20 MINUTES | COOK TIME: 25 MINUTES | SERVES: 6

Inspired by the flavours of Greece, this light and crispy pie will help you put that old bag of spinach in the bottom of your fridge (I know you have some!) to very good use.

INGREDIENTS

300g spinach
2 courgettes, grated
6 cloves of garlic, grated
Salt and pepper
400g feta, crumbled
75g light cream cheese
50g fat-free Greek yoghurt
6 spring onions, finely chopped
15g fresh parsley, finely chopped
3 tbsp finely chopped fresh dill
9 sheets of filo pastry (approx. 190g)
1 egg, beaten
20g sesame seeds

METHOD

1. Add the spinach, courgette, and garlic to a frying pan with some salt and black pepper. Fry until the liquid releases and has been cooked off, then remove the pan from the heat.

2. Once cool enough, squeeze out any excess liquid from the courgette and spinach mixture, then combine it with the feta, cream cheese, Greek yoghurt, spring onions, parsley, and dill. Taste and season this mixture with more salt and black pepper if needed.

3. Spray a baking dish (approx. 20cm x 28cm) with oil, then lay the first piece of filo in so it covers the base. Spray this sheet and then lay two more sheets of filo on top.

4. Add half the cheese mixture to the dish, spread it out evenly, then add three more sheets of filo, spraying with oil between each sheet.

5. Add the remaining cheese mixture and then finish with the final three sheets of filo, again spraying each sheet with oil.

6. Brush the top of the pie with the beaten egg, then sprinkle over the sesame seeds. Cut into six equal slices before baking so you can serve it neatly later.

7. Oven bake at 180°c for 20-25 minutes, until the filling is hot and the pastry is golden and crispy on top.

8. Leave the pie to stand for 10 minutes before taking the slices out, to help them keep their shape. It's delicious served with a Greek tzatziki dip on the side, and a Greek salad too!

Tips: Cutting the dish before it is baked means that you don't lose any of the crispy topping from cutting when you serve it later! If you can't get fresh dill, just use 1 tablespoon of dried dill instead.

CALS:	CARBS:	FAT:	PROTEIN:	DIETARY:
356	22.08G	20.6G	19.6G	VEGGIE

Creamy Mushroom & Spinach Bake

PREP TIME: 5 MINUTES | COOK TIME: 20 MINUTES | SERVES: 4

Another way to use up the forgotten spinach in the bottom of the fridge! With a helping hand from the mighty mushroom, this one is warm, comforting, and on the table in less than 30 minutes.

INGREDIENTS

500g chestnut mushrooms, roughly chopped

1 tbsp paprika

2 tsp black pepper

2 tsp dried oregano

1 tsp dried thyme

1 tsp salt

300ml stock of your choice

1 tbsp cornflour, mixed with cold water

75g light cream cheese

300g spinach

100g mozzarella, grated

50g breadcrumbs

METHOD

1. Fry the mushrooms in an ovenproof pan without any oil until they begin to brown and release some of the liquid in them.

2. Now add some cooking oil spray along with the paprika, black pepper, oregano, thyme, and salt. Stir well for a minute or so.

3. Pour the stock into the pan, bring to a boil and then cook on a high heat for about 5 minutes until it reduces slightly.

4. Add the cornflour paste and stir until thickened, then fold in the cream cheese and spinach. Mix until the spinach has wilted and everything is combined.

5. Top the mushroom mixture with the mozzarella and breadcrumbs, spray with oil and then oven bake at 180°c for about 10 minutes, until the cheese has melted and the breadcrumbs are golden and crispy.

6. There are so many ways to enjoy this bake: with pasta, rice or my personal favourite, crusty bread! I like a slice of sourdough, crisped up in a griddle pan with some cooking oil spray.

Tips: Turn this into a simple pasta bake by adding cooked pasta at the same time as the spinach and cream cheese. I often buy pre-grated mozzarella and keep it in the freezer so it lasts for ages! If you don't mind this not being veggie, beef stock works really well here. You can also get beef flavoured vegetarian stock cubes!

CALS:	CARBS:	FAT:	PROTEIN:	DIETARY:
197	15.8G	8.7G	12.5G	VEGGIE, GF (SKIP THE BREADCRUMBS)

Quiche Stuffed Peppers

PREP TIME: 10 MINUTES | COOK TIME: 40 MINUTES | SERVES: 4

If your bell peppers have seen better days and you need to use up a box of eggs (plus any other bits you can find in the veg drawer) then this one is for you. A great way to clear out the fridge!

INGREDIENTS

8 bell peppers of any colour

6 eggs

75g fat-free Greek yoghurt

75g light cream cheese

2 tsp wholegrain mustard

1 tsp Dijon mustard

2 tsp onion granules

2 tsp garlic granules

200g cheddar, grated

FOR THE FILLING (OPTIONAL)

1 red onion, diced

100g cherry tomatoes, diced

100g broccoli, chopped into small pieces

METHOD

1. First, slice the tops off your bell peppers and take the middles out. Make sure that your peppers will stand up on their own too (I tend to cut a tiny bit off the base of any that don't stand up, just enough so that they have a solid base without making a hole in the bottom).

2. Place the peppers into an ovenproof dish that is just big enough to hold them all standing upright, preferably with high sides so they are supported during cooking.

3. Now make your quiche mixture. Whisk the eggs with the Greek yoghurt, cream cheese, mustards, onion and garlic granules, and 120g of the cheddar.

4. Season the quiche mixture with salt and pepper, then add your chosen fillings. I like to use the offcuts from the bell peppers along with red onion, cherry tomatoes and broccoli – just make sure everything is chopped to roughly the same size.

5. Pour the filling into the peppers and sprinkle the remaining cheese on top, then oven bake at 170°c for 35-45 minutes until the filling is set. You can also air fry these! They should take around 25-30 minutes at 170°c.

Tips: This is just a basic recipe, but you can swap and change the ingredients as needed. Most veg will work in the filling, you can replace the cheddar with something like Red Leicester or feta, and leftover bits of meat like chicken, ham, bacon, or chorizo are all great for throwing in too!

CALS:	CARBS:	FAT:	PROTEIN:	DIETARY:
431	10.1G	28.6G	30.3G	GF, VEGGIE

Sweet Potato Flatbreads

PREP TIME: 20 MINUTES | COOK TIME: 30 MINUTES | SERVES: 4

If you've got some old sweet potatoes hanging around in the back of your cupboard, you can whip up these three-ingredient, delicious, fluffy flatbreads in no time, and freeze them for future use too. I love them with garlicky yoghurt and roasted veggies on top, but the choice is all yours – go wild!

INGREDIENTS

FOR THE FLATBREADS
300g cooked sweet potato (flesh only)
50g fat-free Greek yoghurt
200g self-raising flour

FOR THE ROASTED VEG
1 courgette, sliced
1 red bell pepper, sliced
1 yellow bell pepper, sliced
1 red onion, roughly chopped
100g cherry tomatoes, halved
1 tbsp smoked paprika
1 tbsp dried oregano
Salt and pepper

FOR THE GARLIC YOGHURT
200g fat-free Greek yoghurt
1 clove of garlic, minced
½ lemon, zested and juiced
5g each fresh dill and parsley, to serve
(optional)

METHOD

1. If you don't already have cooked sweet potato (it's a great way to use up leftovers) then start by either microwaving them for around 15-20 minutes, flipping halfway through, or oven baking at 180°c fan for about 30 minutes.

2. Meanwhile, cook your veggies. Spread them all out on a baking tray in a single layer, spray with oil and season generously with the paprika, oregano, salt and pepper, then roast in the oven at 190°c for around 30 minutes.

3. Mash the cooked and cooled sweet potato with the Greek yoghurt, then gradually incorporate the flour with a metal spoon. You can also add a pinch of salt here to taste.

4. Once the mixture begins to form smaller clumps, you can bring it together with your hands. It will be a little sticky but if it feels too wet, add some flour a little at a time. If you think it's too dry, add a little more yoghurt.

5. Keep mixing and kneading the dough for a few minutes, and then leave it to rest for 10 minutes if you have time.

6. Divide the dough into quarters, then flour a rolling pin and roll out each portion into a circle or oval shape about 2cm thick.

7. Get a frying pan nice and hot, spray it with oil and then cook the flatbreads one by one. Turn the heat down to medium once you add the flatbreads and flip them when you see a bubble or two appear on top. Keep them soft and warm under a clean tea towel when cooked.

8. Meanwhile, mix all the ingredients for the garlic yoghurt together in a small bowl and check the roasted veggies are done.

9. Now load up your flatbreads: spread with the garlic yoghurt and then top with the roasted veggies, making sure to spoon over some of the tasty juices from the baking tray!

10. I like to finish my topped flatbreads with chopped fresh herbs, and sometimes add cooked chicken breast too.

Tips: Save the sweet potato skins and throw them in the air fryer or oven with seasonings and oil to make crunchy crisps that are perfect for snacking on, and for topping soups and salads like croutons. You can also cook these flatbreads in the air fryer! They will go super crispy on the outside and fluffy in the centre, more like a pitta than a flatbread.

CALS:	CARBS:	FAT:	PROTEIN:	DIETARY:
289	50.3G	2.1G	13.6G	VEGGIE

FAKEAWAY FRIDAYS

Fridays are for fakeaways! Typically, this is the night when we are exhausted and just want to order a takeaway, so these fusion recipes are all inspired by some of our favourite takeaway dishes, cooked in less time than it would take to get a takeaway delivered! They're super delicious, full of all those flavours that we know and love, without the added grease!

Chicken Tikka Naan Pizzas

PREP TIME: 20 MINUTES | COOK TIME: 20 MINUTES | SERVES: 4

Nothing says 'it's the weekend' like a pizza! These cute little individual pizzas with an Indian twist bring two classic British takeaways together for the perfect Friday night treat.

INGREDIENTS

FOR THE CHICKEN TIKKA

1 heaped tbsp fat-free Greek yoghurt
1 tbsp each tikka paste & tomato purée
2 tsp garlic granules
300g chicken breast, sliced

FOR THE TIKKA MASALA SAUCE

500ml passata
75g fat-free Greek yoghurt
1 tbsp tikka curry powder
1 tbsp onion granules
1 tbsp garlic granules
1 tbsp paprika
2 tsp ground turmeric
1 tsp ground cinnamon

FOR THE NAANS

100g fat-free Greek yoghurt
180g self-raising flour
1 tbsp dried coriander leaf
2 tsp garlic granules
1 tsp baking powder
Pinch of salt

FOR THE TOPPINGS

120g mozzarella, grated
1 bell pepper, sliced
1 red onion, sliced

METHOD

1. For the chicken tikka, combine the yoghurt, tikka paste, tomato purée, and garlic granules in a bowl. Add the sliced chicken and smother in the marinade.

2. Oven bake the chicken at 180°c for around 10-12 minutes, flipping it over halfway through, or air fry for 8 minutes at 180°c. If the chicken isn't 100% cooked after this time, don't worry as it will be cooked again later on the pizza.

3. Meanwhile, make a quick tikka masala sauce by mixing all the ingredients together. Season to taste with salt and sweetener.

4. For the naans, use a metal spoon to fold the yoghurt into the dry ingredients until clumps form, then bring the mixture together with your hands to form a dough.

5. Divide the naan dough into 4 equal balls and then roll them out. Spray a frying pan with oil and cook the naans one at a time for about 3 minutes on each side until golden.

6. Now assemble the pizzas. Spread the naans with the tikka sauce, sprinkle with mozzarella and then top with the tikka chicken, bell pepper and red onion.

7. Oven bake or air fry your pizzas at 180°c for around 5 minutes, until everything is hot and the cheese has melted.

8. I like to drizzle the pizzas with raita and sprinkle some fresh coriander on top. They are also delicious served with Bombay potato style chips!

Tips: If you can get it, I think fat-free coconut yoghurt works even better in the tikka masala sauce. You'll probably make more tikka sauce than you need but it can be kept in the fridge for 5 days or frozen, to be reheated whenever you want for an easy curry or more pizza! You may need to add more yoghurt to the naan dough if it is too stiff. If so, add it gradually in small amounts as you don't want to overdo it.

CALS:	CARBS:	FAT:	PROTEIN:		
441	31.7G	9.9G	39.7G		

Katsu Curry Pasta Bake

PREP TIME: 10 MINUTES | COOK TIME: 40 MINUTES | SERVES: 4

You wouldn't know it, but this recipe is packed with veggies even though it has those indulgent takeaway flavours!

INGREDIENTS

2 white onions, roughly chopped

2 carrots, peeled and roughly chopped

1 thumb-sized piece of ginger, roughly chopped

6 cloves of garlic, roughly chopped

3 tbsp mild curry powder

1 tsp ground turmeric

½ tsp ground cinnamon

350ml chicken stock

½ lime, juiced

3 tbsp light soy sauce

1 tbsp tomato purée

1 tbsp brown sugar

400g chicken breast, thinly sliced

2 tsp garlic granules

1 tsp onion granules

½ tsp white pepper

200g pasta

75g mozzarella, grated

50g breadcrumbs

METHOD

1. Fry the onions, carrots, ginger, and garlic in some cooking oil spray until the onion begins to caramelise on the edges.

2. Add half the curry powder, the turmeric, cinnamon and a pinch of salt to the pan. Stir to coat the veg and then add the stock, lime juice, soy sauce, tomato purée, and brown sugar.

3. Bring the sauce to a boil and allow to simmer with a lid on until the veg is soft, which should take about 20-30 minutes.

4. Meanwhile, coat the chicken with the remaining curry powder, garlic and onion granules, and white pepper. In a separate pan, fry the chicken until cooked through and then set aside. You can also air fry this for about 8 minutes at 180°c.

5. Cook your pasta according to the package instructions in this time too, then drain and set aside.

6. Once the veg in the sauce has softened, use a stick blender or transfer to a food processor and blend until smooth. Add more stock or water here if the sauce is too thick.

7. Mix the katsu sauce with the pasta and chicken in an ovenproof dish. Top with the mozzarella and breadcrumbs, then bake in the oven at 180°c for 10-15 minutes, until the cheese has melted and the breadcrumbs are golden and crispy.

Tips: I like to make the sauce the night before – or a huge batch of it on a weekend – so that I can whip up this pasta bake in no time! I usually make my own breadcrumbs with wholemeal bread, but panko breadcrumbs also work well here.

CALS:	CARBS:	FAT:	PROTEIN:	
485	59.4G	7.7G	44G	

Piri Piri Stuffed Chicken

PREP TIME: 15 MINUTES | COOK TIME: 30 MINUTES | SERVES: 4

We all love that cheeky chicken restaurant in the UK, and this version is even better thanks to a delicious cheesy filling! I like to serve mine with a simple salad.

INGREDIENTS

4 chicken breasts

40g piri piri seasoning (see below)

I yellow bell pepper, thinly sliced

I green bell pepper, thinly sliced

I red bell pepper, thinly sliced

I red onion, thinly sliced

100g cheddar, finely grated

50g light cream cheese

FOR THE PIRI PIRI SEASONING

2 tbsp smoked paprika

2 tbsp onion granules

2 tbsp garlic granules

I tbsp ground coriander

I tbsp dried oregano

I tbsp granulated sugar

I tbsp salt

2 tsp dried parsley

1-2 tsp cayenne pepper (depending on how spicy you like it!)

I tsp ground ginger

METHOD

1. Mix all the ingredients for your piri piri seasoning together first. If you like, double up the quantities to make a second batch for another time!

2. Cut a slit down the side of each chicken breast, making a little pocket inside, then sprinkle over a heaped tablespoon of your piri piri seasoning, spray with oil, and rub all over.

3. To make the filling, first fry the peppers and onion with another heaped tablespoon of the piri piri seasoning until softened, then transfer to a bowl and leave to cool a little.

4. Mix the grated cheese and cream cheese into the spiced veggies, then stuff this mixture into the chicken pockets.

5. Place the stuffed chicken breasts on a baking sheet (or in the air fryer) and bake for 25 minutes, or until the chicken is cooked through (it may take longer depending on the thickness of the chicken breasts).

CALS:	CARBS:	FAT:	PROTEIN:	DIETARY:
315	5.47G	12.4G	40G	GF

Crispy BBQ Bacon Chicken Strips

PREP TIME: 15 MINUTES | COOK TIME: 25 MINUTES | SERVES: 4

Who doesn't love bacon? Who doesn't want chicken coated in bacon crumbs on a Friday night? These are guaranteed to impress and are cooked in no time, perfect for feeding a hungry crowd!

INGREDIENTS

6 smoked bacon medallions

2 tbsp BBQ seasoning

2 tbsp cornflour

75g BBQ sauce

100g golden breadcrumbs

500g chicken breast, cut into thin strips

METHOD

1. Cook the bacon medallions until crispy. I like to air fry them for 6 minutes at 180°c but you can pan fry, grill or oven bake them if you prefer. Set aside to cool.

2. Once the bacon has cooled completely, pulse it in a blender to create the bacon crumb. You can just break it up with your hands or finely chop it with a knife if you don't have a blender.

3. Mix the bacon crumbs with the BBQ seasoning, cornflour and breadcrumbs in a shallow bowl. Dip the chicken strips into the BBQ sauce and then into the bacon crumb mixture.

4. Spray the coated chicken with oil and place on a wire rack above an oven tray, then oven bake at 180°c for 12-15 minutes. Alternatively, you can air fry the chicken at 180°c for about 8 minutes – this is my preferred method as it becomes extra crispy!

5. These are perfect served with more BBQ sauce for dipping, some fries (air fryer fries are the best!) and corn on the cob on the side.

Tips: You should get about 4-6 pieces of chicken per person, depending on how big you cut the strips. Make sure not to drench your chicken in the BBQ sauce, or the bacon crumb won't stick. You just need a thin coating on each piece, so less is more!

CALS:	CARBS:	FAT:	PROTEIN:	DIETARY:
385	35G	4.1G	50.6G	DF, GF (USE GF BREADCRUMBS)

Sticky Beef Noodles

PREP TIME: 10 MINUTES | COOK TIME: 15 MINUTES | SERVES: 4

A 15 minute fakeaway: with this recipe, you have no excuses for calling the takeaway! It all comes together conveniently in one pan too, so there's not even much washing up to do afterwards.

INGREDIENTS

500ml beef stock

50g hoisin sauce

50ml dark soy sauce

3 tbsp honey

1 tbsp sesame oil

1 lime, juiced

500g lean beef mince

300g mushrooms, diced

1 small red onion, diced

6 spring onions, finely sliced, greens and whites separated

6 cloves of garlic, grated

2 tsp grated fresh ginger

1 red chilli, sliced (optional)

200g dried noodles (I like egg noodles)

1 x 225g tin of bamboo shoots, drained

1 x 225g tin of water chestnuts, drained

METHOD

1. Start by making the sauce. Mix the beef stock, hoisin sauce, dark soy sauce, honey, sesame oil, and lime juice together in a jug, then set aside.

2. Fry the beef mince with some cooking oil spray until beginning to brown, then add the mushrooms, red onion, and spring onion whites.

3. Once that begins to soften, add the garlic, ginger, and chilli if using. Let that become fragrant, then push everything right to the edge of the pan so that you have a large well in the middle.

4. Add the dried noodles and sauce to the middle of the pan, cook until the noodles are soft, then add the bamboo shoots, water chestnuts, and spring onion greens (or save for garnish).

5. Mix everything together until the noodles are combined, then serve immediately. If you didn't add the spring onion greens earlier, sprinkle these over the top.

6. Sesame seeds are nice as a garnish too and prawn crackers on the side are a must – perfect for scooping up all that sticky beef! If you fancy even more veg, steamed pak choi or tenderstem broccoli work well with this.

Tips: I love water chestnuts and bamboo shoots in a stir fry, but you can use whatever veg you like here. Any dried noodles will work in this recipe. I've often used noodles from a packet of instant ramen when I haven't got anything else!

CALS:	CARBS:	FAT:	PROTEIN:	DIETARY:
495	65.4G	8.6G	30.8G	DF

Samosa Burritos

PREP TIME: 15 MINUTES | COOK TIME: 25 MINUTES | SERVES: 4

The last thing you want on a Friday night is fuss; this recipe has all the flavour of a delicious samosa filling without the hassle of wrapping them up perfectly!

INGREDIENTS

FOR THE BURRITO

3 medium potatoes, peeled and diced into small cubes

1 white onion, diced

4 cloves of garlic, grated

1 tsp grated fresh ginger

500g lean beef mince

1 tbsp mild curry powder

1 tbsp dried coriander leaf

1 tsp ground turmeric

1 tsp ground cumin

1 tsp salt

2 carrots, peeled and finely diced

100g frozen peas

4 tortilla wraps

FOR THE RAITA

200g fat-free Greek yoghurt

2 cloves of garlic, grated

5g fresh mint, finely chopped

5g fresh coriander, finely chopped

150g cucumber, grated and squeezed out

METHOD

1. Boil the diced potato in salted water until beginning to soften, then drain and set aside. This should only take 5 minutes, if that.

2. In a frying pan with some cooking oil spray, fry the onion, garlic and ginger until the onion begins to colour.

3. Add the beef mince, curry powder, dried coriander, turmeric, cumin, and salt to the pan. Fry until the beef has some colour and the spices are mixed through.

4. Add the carrots, peas and potatoes to the beef mixture and cook until they have softened.

5. Meanwhile, make the raita by mixing the yoghurt with the garlic, fresh herbs, and grated cucumber. You might need to season it with a pinch of salt to taste.

6. Load up your tortilla wraps with the raita and beef filling, then fold and roll up tightly.

7. If you can be bothered, wrap the burritos in foil and oven bake or air fry them until warmed through. However, you can eat them without this step if you can't wait!

8. There's not much I think you need to add to this as everything is in the burrito! I just serve them with a little bit of extra raita and a salad on the side. If I'm extra hungry, I'll make some pilau rice too which goes amazingly well with the other fillings.

Tips: You can actually use the beef mixture to make samosas using the traditional wrappers, or sometimes I cheat and use filo pastry! This is also lovely served 'burrito bowl' style, with pilau rice, salad, mango chutney and raita. Sometimes I add a lamb stock cube to make it taste more like the usual lamb filling of a samosa, just without all the fat!

CALS:	CARBS:	FAT:	PROTEIN:	DIETARY:
461	30.8G	8.7G	37.7G	DF (SKIP THE RAITA)

Sticky Orange Gammon

PREP TIME: 10 MINUTES | COOK TIME: 15 MINUTES | SERVES: 4

Gammon steaks with fried eggs and pineapple are delicious, but here's something different to do with them when you fancy a change! This meal is on the table in under 30 minutes, and I love it with boiled or egg fried rice (which I like to sneak cauliflower into!) and more stir fried veggies.

INGREDIENTS

2 large oranges, zested and juiced

4 cloves of garlic, grated

2 tsp grated fresh ginger

4 tbsp light soy sauce

2 tbsp honey

½ tsp Chinese five spice

¼ tsp ground cinnamon

¼ tsp fennel seeds, ground

2 gammon steaks, sliced (approx. 400g)

100g mangetout

1 red bell pepper, roughly chopped

1 yellow bell pepper, roughly chopped

½ green bell pepper, roughly chopped

2 tsp cornflour

METHOD

1. Combine the orange juice and zest, garlic, ginger, soy sauce, honey, Chinese five spice, cinnamon, and fennel in a mixing jug, then top up with around 200ml of boiling water.

2. Add a sprinkle of Chinese five spice to the sliced gammon and then lightly fry in cooking spray oil.

3. Once the gammon has some colour and is almost cooked through, throw in the mangetout and chopped peppers. Stir fry for a minute or so until they begin to soften at the edges.

4. Pour the orange juice mixture into the pan and cook on a high heat until it starts to reduce and become sticky.

5. Mix the cornflour with a little cold water to make a smooth paste, then add this to the sauce and stir well to thicken it up even further.

6. Make sure the gammon is fully cooked and then serve up immediately!

Tips: If you use sesame oil as your cooking spray, you'll get a really nice nutty flavour that will remind you of a takeaway! Always zest your citrus fruits before juicing them, as it's much easier to do this way round. You can swap the veg here for whatever you like – just use up what you have! This recipe also works well with chicken, pork, or meat substitutes like tofu.

CALS:	CARBS:	FAT:	PROTEIN:	DIETARY:
229	21.2G	5.8G	22.1G	GF, DF

Sweet & Sour Pork Skewers

PREP TIME: 15 MINUTES | COOK TIME: 20 MINUTES | SERVES: 4

This recipe turns a takeaway favourite into fun finger food that the whole family can enjoy! Why not try making the skewers together so that everyone can customise theirs?

INGREDIENTS

400g lean diced pork
4 tbsp light soy sauce
4 tbsp dark soy sauce
1 tsp garlic granules
1 tsp onion granules
½ tsp bicarbonate of soda
2 tbsp tomato purée
4 cloves of garlic, grated
2 tsp grated fresh ginger
150ml chicken stock
3 tbsp balsamic vinegar
2 tbsp honey
1 tsp Chinese five spice
1 tbsp cornflour, mixed with cold water
250g pineapple, cut into chunks
2 red onions, cut into chunks
1 red bell pepper, cut into chunks
1 green bell pepper, cut into chunks

TO SERVE (OPTIONAL)
Sliced spring onion
Sesame seeds

METHOD

1. First, marinate the meat. Mix the pork with 1 tablespoon of each soy sauce, the garlic and onion granules, bicarbonate of soda, and half the tomato purée, then set aside.

2. Now make the sticky glaze. Combine the grated garlic and ginger, chicken stock, balsamic vinegar, honey, five spice, and the remaining soy sauces and tomato purée in a pan.

3. Cook on a high heat until this mixture becomes sticky and thickened, then stir in the cornflour paste to thicken it a little bit more. Split the glaze into 2 portions and set aside.

4. Load up the skewers with the marinated pork, pineapple, onion, and bell peppers. Brush them with one portion of the glaze (you won't use it all yet).

5. Oven bake or air fry the skewers at 180°c for 10-12 minutes, flipping and glazing them every couple of minutes. You can also do this on the barbecue!

6. Once the meat and veg are cooked through, serve the skewers with more of the glaze drizzled over. Use the second portion for this, that hasn't been contaminated by the brush that touched the raw meat. I also like to sprinkle them with sesame seeds and spring onions.

7. These are perfect with boiled or egg fried rice, and lots of greens cooked in sesame oil and soy sauce!

Tips: It's really important to split the glaze into two portions, keeping one for glazing the meat during cooking, and one just for drizzling over at the end, to avoid any contamination from the raw meat.

CALS:	CARBS:	FAT:	PROTEIN:	DIETARY:	
248	31.1G	1.6G	25G	DF	

Cajun Salmon Burgers

PREP TIME: 15 MINUTES | COOK TIME: 20 MINUTES | SERVES: 4

It's tempting to make the same dish every time when it comes to fish, but these Cajun salmon burgers give the classic beef burger a run for its money! They're packed with flavour and super juicy, everything a burger should be.

INGREDIENTS

FOR THE SALMON BURGERS
500g salmon fillets, skin removed
1 small white onion, roughly chopped
1 roasted red pepper (see tips)
4 cloves of garlic, peeled
½ lemon, zested and juiced
3 tbsp Cajun seasoning
50g breadcrumbs

FOR THE LEMON 'AIOLI'
4 tbsp light mayonnaise
4 tbsp fat-free Greek yoghurt
2 small cloves of garlic, grated
½ lemon, zested and juiced

TO SERVE
4 burger buns (wholemeal works well)
Your preferred salad (red onion, lettuce, tomato, cucumber, and avocado are all good options)

METHOD

1. Put the salmon into a food processor with the onion, roasted red pepper, garlic cloves, lemon zest and juice, Cajun seasoning, and breadcrumbs.

2. Pulse until you have a smooth mixture. You don't want it to be too smooth or sticky, so keep an eye on it.

3. Shape the mixture into 4 equally sized patties of about 2cm thickness, then oven bake for around 20 minutes at 180°c, flipping them over halfway through.

4. Alternatively, you can air fry the patties and I actually prefer this, with the added bonus that it takes less time (about 15 minutes) and I don't usually bother flipping them either.

5. Meanwhile, make your lemon aioli by mixing the mayo, yoghurt, garlic, lemon zest, and lemon juice together.

6. This is also a great time to prep anything else you might want on your burger, such as slicing your salad and toasting your buns in a dry pan (to stop them going soggy when you pile up your burger!).

7. Once your salmon patties are cooked, load everything up! Spread your toasted buns with the lemony aioli, then add your salad of choice (I like sliced avocado, red onion and tomato) and finally add the Cajun salmon patties to complete your burgers.

Tips: For the roasted red pepper, you can roast your own (which is always best, but time consuming!) or use roasted pepper from a jar. If jarred, I always prefer the ones in oil to brine, but either way, drain and rinse them before adding!

CALS:	CARBS:	FAT:	PROTEIN:	DIETARY:
482	44.5G	21.1G	36.9G	GF (USE GF BUNS), DF (SKIP THE YOGHURT)

Honey Garlic Prawns

PREP TIME: 5 MINUTES | COOK TIME: 10 MINUTES | SERVES: 4

This easy, sweet and sticky sauce comes together in just 10 minutes, so much faster than a takeaway and, dare I say, far more delicious too!

INGREDIENTS

400g raw king prawns

75ml light soy sauce

1 tbsp sesame oil

100ml honey

8 cloves of garlic, diced

2 tsp grated fresh ginger

1 red bell pepper, roughly chopped

1 green bell pepper, roughly chopped

TO SERVE (OPTIONAL)

Sliced spring onion

Sesame seeds

METHOD

1. Mix the prawns with 2 tablespoons of the soy sauce, some black pepper, and the sesame oil.

2. In a separate bowl, mix the remaining soy sauce with the honey, garlic and ginger.

3. In a pan, fry the chopped peppers first until they begin to soften slightly.

4. Drain any excess liquid off the prawns, then add them to the pan. Once they start to turn pink (this should only take a couple of minutes), pour in the sauce.

5. Turn the heat up high and cook until the sauce is sticky, clinging to the peppers and prawns. Make sure the prawns are fully cooked but don't overdo them as they will become tough.

6. I like to sprinkle sliced spring onion and sesame seeds all over the prawns just before serving. I particularly like them with boiled or egg fried rice, but noodles work too if you prefer. Pan fried pak choi or crispy kale are also great accompaniments.

Tips: You can use cooked prawns in this recipe; just add the prawns to the pan right at the end (after the sauce) so they don't overcook and become tough. It also works well with chicken, salmon or pork!

CALS:	CARBS:	FAT:	PROTEIN:	DIETARY:
205	26G	1.5G	21.3G	DF

SOCIAL SATURDAYS

Whatever you're up to on a Saturday night – a dinner party, date night, or family night in – these recipes have got you covered. Some of them require a little more prep that you might like to avoid during the week, but when you've got the luxury of time on your hands, they're worth every step!

Lemony Chicken Kiev

PREP TIME: 20 MINUTES, PLUS 2 HOURS FREEZING | COOK TIME: 25 MINUTES | SERVES: 4

A bright, zesty twist on the family favourite. This recipe requires a tiny bit of prep in advance, but it's so worth it!

INGREDIENTS

50g light butter

2 lemons, zested

5g fresh parsley

1 tsp grated garlic

150g breadcrumbs

1 tbsp dried oregano

1 tsp garlic granules

1 tsp onion granules

1 tsp salt

1 tsp black pepper

4 chicken breasts

2 eggs, beaten

METHOD

1. This first step needs to be done at least 2 hours before you want to make the recipe. I recommend doing it the night before! Combine the butter, zest of 1 lemon, parsley, and garlic, then squeeze in about a quarter of the juice from the lemon you zested. Place the flavoured butter on a piece of cling film and roll into a sausage shape. Flatten so you have more of an oblong, then freeze for a minimum of 2 hours.

2. Mix the breadcrumbs with the oregano, garlic and onion granules, salt and pepper, and zest of the other lemon (don't discard this lemon once it's zested!), then set aside.

3. Slice a pocket around 4cm long into the centre of each chicken breast. Take your flavoured butter out of the freezer and slice into 4 equal pieces, placing one in each pocket.

4. Dip each stuffed chicken breast into the beaten egg, let the excess drip off, and then dip into the breadcrumb mixture until fully coated, double dipping if you have excess crumbs.

5. Place the stuffed and coated chicken breasts onto a baking tray or into an air fryer sprayed with oil and give the tops a spritz of oil too.

6. Cook at 190°c for around 20-25 minutes, until chicken is cooked through and crumbs are golden and crispy. This will likely be closer to the 20-minute mark if using an air fryer.

7. These go really well with mash or chips and greens or salad. To serve, cut the lemon that you zested for the breadcrumbs into 4 wedges and squeeze them over the dish.

Tips: The flavoured butter in this recipe is also great stirred into pasta and melted over steak or fish!

CALS:	CARBS:	FAT:	PROTEIN:	
269	28.9G	12.4G	43.5G	

'Marry Me' Chicken Lasagne

PREP TIME: 20 MINUTES | COOK TIME: 35 MINUTES | SERVES: 6

This is the perfect date night dinner; what could be a better way of showing someone you care than lovingly preparing each layer of this deliciously indulgent dish? They don't call it 'marry me' lasagne for nothing!

INGREDIENTS

FOR THE 'MARRY ME' SAUCE
120g sundried tomatoes, drained of any oil
8 shallots, finely diced
8 cloves of garlic, grated
1 large courgette, grated
500g chicken mince
1 tbsp dried oregano
1 tbsp smoked paprika
50g tomato purée
400g tinned chopped tomatoes
200ml chicken stock
½ lemon, juiced
300g spinach
75g light cream cheese

FOR THE WHITE SAUCE
240ml milk (I use skimmed)
1 tsp onion granules
1 tsp garlic granules
1 tsp dried oregano
1 tbsp cornflour
30g parmesan, grated

FOR THE ASSEMBLY
250g fresh lasagne sheets
50g mozzarella, grated
30g parmesan, grated

METHOD

1. Fry the sundried tomatoes, shallots, garlic, and courgette on a medium-low heat with a pinch of salt until the onions are softened and translucent.

2. Add the chicken mince, oregano, smoked paprika, and tomato purée to the pan and stir until the chicken mince is beginning to colour.

3. Add the tinned tomatoes, chicken stock and lemon juice. Stir well, pop a lid on the pan and allow to simmer for around 45-60 minutes, checking occasionally to make sure the liquid isn't evaporating too quickly and adding more if needed.

4. Once the sauce has reduced a little, fold in the spinach and cream cheese, then set aside to cool.

5. Meanwhile, make your white sauce. Heat the milk in a saucepan with the onion granules, garlic granules, oregano, and a few twists of black pepper.

6. Mix the cornflour with 1 tablespoon of cold water to make a smooth paste, then add this to the warm milk and stir continuously until it thickens slightly.

7. Finally, stir in the grated parmesan and mix well until you have a smooth sauce.

8. Now it's time to assemble your lasagne. In a baking dish approximately 25cm x 20cm (don't worry if you don't have the exact size) start with a layer of the chicken sauce, cover with lasagne sheets, then pour over some of the white sauce and spread it out evenly.

9. Repeat this process twice, so you have 3 layers of everything in total, then finish with the last of the white sauce. Sprinkle the mozzarella and remaining parmesan on top.

10. Oven bake the lasagne for 20 minutes at 180°c fan until everything is cooked through, and the cheese on top is golden.

11. Leave it to stand for a minimum of 5-10 minutes before serving. This will help the lasagne keep its shape, but it will still be hot.

12. Serve your lasagne with a side salad, and some garlic bread if you're extra hungry!

Tips: If using dried lasagne sheets, you can either soak them in boiling water before using (spray them with oil first so they don't stick together) or increase the baking time to 40 minutes and cover the dish with foil until the last 5-10 minutes. When layering your lasagne, make sure your fillings have cooled a little after cooking. This will help the layers stay in place once baked.

CALS:	CARBS:	FAT:	PROTEIN:	DIETARY:
395	35.9G	13G	32.1G	GF

Balsamic & Red Wine Glazed Steak

PREP TIME: 5 MINUTES | COOK TIME: 15 MINUTES | SERVES: 2

Elevate your steak night with this simple twist that's easy to execute but guaranteed to impress!

INGREDIENTS

2 x 200g rump steaks, trimmed of fat
75ml balsamic vinegar
75ml red wine
2 tsp light butter
2 cloves of garlic, smashed
2 sprigs of fresh rosemary
Salt and black pepper

METHOD

1. Season the steaks with salt and pepper on both sides, then pan fry to your liking. For medium rare you'll need about 3-4 minutes on each side; for medium you'll need 4-6 minutes on each side, and for well-done you'll need about 2-4 minutes on each side at first, then another 4-6 minutes after flipping again.

2. Once the steaks are cooked to your liking, place on a warm plate and cover with foil.

3. In the same pan, cook the balsamic vinegar, wine, butter, garlic, and rosemary on a high heat until the wine cooks off and you're left with a slightly thicker liquid.

4. Add the rested steaks to the pan and cook for up to a minute on each side, spooning the glaze all over them as you go.

5. Set the pan aside while you plate up your sides. You can't beat chips, tenderstem broccoli and asparagus for a steak dinner in my opinion! I love mushrooms fried with garlic too.

6. I like to slice my steak before serving but you can leave it whole if preferred. Drizzle any glaze left in the pan over your steaks to finish the dish and enjoy.

Tips: You can use whatever cuts of steak you prefer – sirloin, ribeye, fillet, etc. – but rump is actually the cheapest and the lowest in calories too! It also has a lot of flavour, so it's perfect for this dish. I usually trim the fat before and after cooking.

CALS:	CARBS:	FAT:	PROTEIN:	DIETARY:
426	8.1G	22.9G	40.6G	GF

Parmesan Pork Schnitzel

PREP TIME: 10 MINUTES | COOK TIME: 15 MINUTES | SERVES: 4

Because this is so quick and easy to prepare, it's great for when you have guests over – so you can spend more time being the perfect host, rather than slaving away in the kitchen!

INGREDIENTS

4 pork loin medallions
100g golden breadcrumbs
50g parmesan, grated
1 tbsp dried parsley
2 tsp paprika
½ tsp salt
½ tsp white pepper
2 eggs, beaten

METHOD

1. Trim any fat off your pork medallions, then place them on a large chopping board and cover with cling film. Bash with a rolling pin or a meat tenderiser if you have one until the medallions are half their original thickness and all equal in size.

2. Mix the breadcrumbs, parmesan, parsley, paprika, salt, and white pepper together. Dip the pork into the beaten egg and then the breadcrumbs, double dipping if you have any extra.

3. Place the breadcrumbed pork on a baking tray lined with greaseproof paper and sprayed with oil, then spray the tops so the coating doesn't burn.

4. Bake the schnitzel at 190°c for around 15 minutes, flipping them over halfway through. You can cook these in the air fryer too – you won't need greaseproof paper, and you shouldn't need to flip them either – which will take 10-12 minutes at 190°c.

5. This schnitzel is lovely with a salad in a lemony dressing if you want a lighter meal. For something heartier, I usually do mustard mash or lemon and thyme roasted potatoes with greens and carrots. It's also lovely with a creamy mushroom or peppercorn sauce.

Tips: You can make this recipe with chicken, which will cook in a similar amount of time, and for a veggie option I've made it with cauliflower 'steaks' before too! You can use any breadcrumbs for the coating. I like homemade ones made from wholemeal bread, but crushed cornflakes or panko breadcrumbs also work well.

CALS:	CARBS:	FAT:	PROTEIN:
299	18.9G	8.8G	35G

Sausage Pasta Shells in Roasted Tomato Sauce

PREP TIME: 25 MINUTES | COOK TIME: 50 MINUTES | SERVES: 4

Unlike other speedy pasta dishes, this one is a labour of love, but the result is an elevated pasta dish bursting with deep, rich flavours. It looks gorgeous in the centre of the table too!

INGREDIENTS

1kg tomatoes, chopped into chunks
50ml balsamic vinegar
2 large sprigs of fresh rosemary
4 tsp dried oregano
2 tsp dried basil
1 tsp black pepper
½ tsp salt
16 conchiglioni (giant pasta shells)
8 cloves of garlic, finely chopped
6 shallots, finely diced
6 good quality pork sausages
1 tsp fennel seeds
1 tsp dried thyme
10g fresh basil, finely chopped
5g fresh parsley, finely chopped
300g ricotta
20g parmesan, grated

METHOD

1. Place the tomatoes in a baking dish, spray with oil and then add the balsamic vinegar, rosemary, half the oregano, the basil, black pepper, and salt.

2. Toss to combine the tomatoes with all the seasoning and then roast in the oven at 180°c for around 30 minutes.

3. Meanwhile, boil the pasta shells in heavily salted water until al dente, which should take around 12 minutes. Drain and arrange in one layer on a tray lined with greaseproof paper and sprayed with oil to stop the pasta sticking together.

4. To make the filling, first fry the garlic and shallots in some cooking oil spray until softened and coloured. Once they're soft, remove half from the pan and save for later.

5. Remove the sausages from their skins and add to the pan with the remaining shallots and garlic. Break up the sausage meat with a wooden spoon until you have lots of smaller crumbled up bits and cook these until they start to brown.

6. Season the sausage mixture with the remaining oregano, fennel seeds, thyme, and salt and black pepper to taste.

7. Take the pan off the heat and stir in the fresh basil, parsley, and ricotta. Use a teaspoon to stuff the pasta shells with this mixture until they are all evenly filled.

8. Remove the roasted tomatoes from the oven, discard the rosemary sprigs, and crush with a fork. Mix in the reserved shallots and garlic, then season to taste with salt, black pepper and sugar as needed. Spread the sauce out evenly in the baking dish.

9. Arrange the stuffed pasta shells neatly in the tomato sauce, top with the parmesan and then cover the dish with foil.

10. Bake at 180°c for 10 minutes, then remove the foil and bake for another 10 minutes. This has to be served with garlic ciabatta to mop up the delicious sauce! A fresh, peppery rocket salad pairs perfectly with the rich flavours of this dish too.

Tips: Add a little olive oil to your pasta water while you cook the shells to stop them from sticking together in the water, and make sure you use a really big pot! Make sure the sausage mixture isn't too hot before you add the ricotta, or it will be more difficult to stuff into your shells.

CALS:	CARBS:	FAT:	PROTEIN:
496	51.6G	19.3G	27G

Stuffed Pork Tenderloin

PREP TIME: 25 MINUTES | COOK TIME: 45 MINUTES | SERVES: 4

With its perfect swirls, this dish looks so pretty plated up: the perfect dinner party or date night showstopper. Although it looks impressive, it's actually pretty easy to pull together!

INGREDIENTS

50g chopped hazelnuts

4 shallots, finely diced

4 cloves of garlic, crushed

100g chestnut mushrooms, finely diced

150g spinach, finely chopped

2 roasted red peppers, diced

½ lemon, juiced

30g parmesan, grated

1 heaped tbsp light cream cheese

1 tbsp dried oregano

2 tsp dried basil

1 tsp dried rosemary

½ tsp dried thyme

1 tsp black pepper

1 pork tenderloin fillet (450-500g)

5-6 slices of Parma ham

METHOD

1. Toast the hazelnuts in a dry pan, stirring often. Once they have some colour, add some cooking oil spray and the shallots, garlic, and mushrooms.

2. Fry until the shallots and mushrooms have some colour, then add the spinach, roasted peppers, lemon juice, parmesan, cream cheese, oregano, basil, rosemary, thyme, and black pepper. Stir well and then set aside to cool.

3. Place the pork tenderloin fillet on a large chopping board and slice through the middle lengthways, taking care not to cut all the way through. We are aiming to butterfly the tenderloin, like you would with chicken breast.

4. Place a piece of cling film over the pork and bash with a rolling pin or meat tenderiser if you have one, until it's about 1cm thick and doubled in width.

5. Spread the vegetable filling all over the flattened pork, then carefully and tightly roll up the pork lengthways so you have a long, thin sausage shape.

6. Wrap the Parma ham around the pork, making sure the seam is tightly joined on the underside of the roll, and place the whole thing in a roasting tin.

7. Cover the tin with foil and bake at 180°c for 20 minutes, then remove the foil and bake for another 10-20 minutes until the pork is cooked through (this will depend on how thinly you flattened the pork earlier).

8. Remove from the oven and leave to rest with the foil placed loosely back over the top for 10 minutes before carving into 8 slices.

9. This is delicious served with mashed potatoes and mushroom gravy, plus your favourite vegetables. I always like greens, and cauliflower cheese goes nicely too! For a fresh summery twist, I like to serve it with herby air fried potatoes and salad.

Tips: You need to make sure everything is wrapped really tightly with this one to get the lovely swirl effect when sliced. If needed, you can secure the pork and Parma ham in place with cocktail sticks or use cooking twine to keep everything together.

CALS:	CARBS:	FAT:	PROTEIN:	DIETARY:
340	6.4G	17.2G	37.8G	GF

Mediterranean Lamb Traybake

PREP TIME: 20 MINUTES | COOK TIME: 1 HOUR 40 MINUTES | SERVES: 6

The rich flavours in this traybake make it the star of the show. It takes some time for the delicious flavours to marry in the oven, but it's so worth it for the tender lamb at the end.

INGREDIENTS

½ leg of lamb (around 900g)

2 white onions, finely diced

8 cloves of garlic, roughly chopped

2 bell peppers, roughly chopped

800g tinned chopped tomatoes

150ml lamb stock

100ml red wine

2 bay leaves

2 tbsp dried oregano

2 tsp dried thyme

Salt and pepper

75g green olives, drained and roughly chopped

10g fresh parsley

1 lemon

METHOD

1. Trim off all the visible fat from the leg of lamb. Season it with salt and pepper, then sear in a hot pan until golden on all sides. Remove from the pan and set aside.

2. In the same pan, add some cooking oil spray if needed and fry the onions, garlic, and peppers. Once they have softened, tip them into a large baking dish.

3. Add the tinned tomatoes, stock, wine, bay leaves, oregano, and thyme to the dish. Season to taste with salt and black pepper, then stir everything together.

4. Sit the lamb leg on top of the sauce, cover the dish with foil and roast for 1 hour at 160°c. Remove the foil, increase the oven temperature to 180°c and roast for another 30 minutes.

5. Once the lamb is tender, add the olives and parsley immediately after removing the dish from the oven. Halve the lemon and squeeze the juice all over.

6. You don't need much to serve with this, though fresh bread to mop everything up goes nicely! If you prefer, you can also serve the lamb with a salad and some crispy potatoes.

Tips: If you can get tinned cherry tomatoes, they add a lovely sweet touch to this dish. If you want to serve 6-8 people, use a whole leg of lamb but keep all the other quantities the same. Any leftovers make a delicious sauce for pasta! You can also make this in the slow cooker; it should be perfect after 6-8 hours on low.

CALS:	CARBS:	FAT:	PROTEIN:	DIETARY:	
395	14.5G	10.7G	56.1G	GF (CHECK THE STOCK CUBE), DF	

Honey Harissa Stuffed Salmon

PREP TIME: 15 MINUTES | COOK TIME: 25 MINUTES | SERVES: 4

Salmon is such a versatile fish, and one that most people enjoy. It's easy to become stuck in a rut, seasoning it with the same old flavours like the classic lemon and dill, but this sweet and slightly spicy recipe will leave a lasting impression!

INGREDIENTS

75g light cream cheese

3 tbsp harissa paste

1 roasted red pepper, diced

3 cloves of garlic, grated

1 lemon, zested and juiced

2 tsp dried oregano

4 fillets of salmon

1 tbsp smoked paprika

1 tsp black pepper

½ tsp salt

2 tbsp honey

METHOD

1. Combine the cream cheese with half the harissa paste, the roasted red pepper, garlic, lemon zest and juice, oregano, and some salt and pepper to taste.

2. Rub the salmon fillets with the smoked paprika, black pepper, and salt. Working with one at a time, turn the salmon on its side and cut a pocket into the thicker part, making sure not to cut all the way through. Stuff these pockets with the cream cheese mixture.

3. Mix the remaining harissa paste with the honey and brush this all over the salmon. If oven baking, place the salmon fillets on a baking tray lined with baking paper.

4. Bake at 180°c for 12-15 minutes in the oven or 10-12 minutes in the air fryer, until the salmon is cooked through (thicker fillets may need a few more minutes).

5. In the summer, this is really good with a couscous and chickpea salad packed with a rainbow of fresh herbs and vegetables like peppers, tomatoes, cucumber, and carrots. For a cosy meal on a cold evening, it also goes well with wild rice or crispy potatoes, and roasted carrots.

Tips: This isn't too spicy at all because of the cream cheese and honey, but if you want to make it even milder, you can swap the harissa paste in the filling with tomato purée, and just have the harissa glaze on top.

CALS:	CARBS:	FAT:	PROTEIN:	DIETARY:
305	10.7G	17.3G	25.5G	GF

Sour Cream & Onion Fish Bites

PREP TIME: 20 MINUTES | COOK TIME: 10 MINUTES | SERVES: 4

Who doesn't love crispy fish? These delicious little bites are perfect for sharing with a crowd, and the sour cream and onion flavour complements the fish so well. Kids and grown-ups will love them!

INGREDIENTS

100g sour cream and onion crisps
2 tbsp cornflour
2 tsp onion granules
1 tsp black pepper
500g cod loin
2 tbsp plain flour
2 eggs, beaten

METHOD

1. Crush the crisps. I usually just squish them in the bag, but you can blend them in a food processor, or bash them with the end of a rolling pin in a bowl.

2. Mix the crisps with the cornflour, onion granules and black pepper.

3. Cut the cod loin into bite-size pieces, either fingers or smaller cubes, then sprinkle the plain flour over them and toss to coat.

4. Dip the floured fish into the beaten egg and then the crushed crisps until all the pieces are coated. Don't worry if there are little gaps! Double dip if you have any spare crisp coating.

5. Place the bites on a tray lined with greaseproof paper, spray them with oil and then oven bake at 180°c for about 10-12 minutes. If the fish fillets were thin or you have cut them into smaller pieces, reduce the cooking time by a couple of minutes.

6. You can also cook these in the air fryer. You won't need greaseproof paper, and they should only take about 8 minutes at 180°c.

7. These are best served with chips, of course: you can't beat fish and chips. Peas are a delicious accompaniment too; whether you go for the garden or mushy variety is up to you!

8. I also love to dip these bites into soured cream mixed with finely chopped fresh chives to really enhance the sour cream and onion flavour.

Tips: I prefer to use a lighter crisp here, like Popchips or Sunbites, but Pringles work well too!

CALS:	CARBS:	FAT:	PROTEIN:	DIETARY:
312	27G	8.6G	30.4G	DF

Baked Pizza Spinach Gnocchi

PREP TIME: 30 MINUTES | COOK TIME: 20 MINUTES | SERVES: 4

Making your own gnocchi is easier than you think but it's always impressive. This meal is a great way to pack in some veggies, even though it tastes like you're eating pizza!

INGREDIENTS

750g floury potatoes (like Maris Piper or King Edward)
400g spinach
150g plain flour
½ tsp salt
500g passata
75ml balsamic vinegar
1 tbsp dried oregano
1 tbsp dried basil
Salt and black pepper
Pinch of sugar

TOPPINGS

75g mozzarella, grated
Pepperoni slices
Red onion, finely sliced
Bell pepper, finely sliced
Fresh basil leaves

METHOD

1. Prick your potatoes with a fork and microwave them for about 15-20 minutes, flipping halfway through, until they're fluffy in the middle.

2. Meanwhile, add the spinach to a pan of boiling water and cook for up to 5 minutes until wilted. Drain and squeeze out the excess liquid, then finely chop by hand or in a food processor.

3. Once the potatoes are just cool enough to handle, slice them in half and scoop out the insides. Press them through a potato ricer if you have one, or mash until light and fluffy.

4. Combine the potato, chopped spinach, flour, and salt in a bowl with your hands until a dough forms. If it seems too sticky, keep gradually adding flour (it will depend on how much liquid you squeezed out of your spinach earlier) until you have a pliable dough.

5. Cut the dough into 4 equal pieces and roll them into long sausage shapes. Cut these into little pillow-shaped gnocchi.

6. Pan fry the gnocchi in some cooking oil spray until a little crispy and golden.

7. Meanwhile, make your pizza sauce. Add the passata, balsamic vinegar, and herbs to a pan. Bring to the boil, then simmer on a gentle heat to infuse all the flavours. Taste and season with salt, black pepper and sugar if needed.

8. Mix the pizza sauce and gnocchi together in an ovenproof dish, top with the grated mozzarella and then add any other pizza toppings you fancy. I always like slices of pepperoni, and sometimes vegetables like peppers and onions too.

9. Bake in the oven at 180°c for about 10 minutes, until the cheese is golden and bubbling and everything is piping hot.

10. I like to finish the pizza gnocchi with some black pepper and fresh basil, then serve it with a big bowl of fresh rocket, tomato and balsamic salad, or sometimes a Caesar salad. Garlic bread is always a winner if you want to bulk it out with some more carbs too!

Tips: If you want to cheat a little in this recipe, you can use readymade or leftover mash for the gnocchi. Just make sure it's warm when you use it, as this makes the gnocchi extra soft. You can also boil, bake or air fry your potatoes instead of microwaving them, and if air frying or baking you can save the crispy skins for a snack (or the taco shells on page 92).

CALS:	CARBS:	FAT:	PROTEIN:	DIETARY:	
372	69.6G	7.7G	14.8G	VEGGIE (WITHOUT PEPPERONI)	

SAUCY SUNDAYS

Everyone loves a 'Sunday reset' and it's also a great time to reset your fridge and freezer with these handy sauces and sides. The recipes in this chapter will come in handy for last-minute dinners, lunches and snacks, making meal prep easier throughout the week when you have less time to cook.

Pesto

PREP TIME: 10 MINUTES | COOK TIME: 5 MINUTES | SERVES: 16 (1 TBSP SERVINGS)

Pesto is a kitchen staple for many, and with good reason! This versatile sauce can be mixed into pasta, mash or grains to create a delicious side. It's amazing as a dip, can be mixed with mayo or butter to create the ultimate condiment, and is useful for marinating meats, fish and veggies too!

INGREDIENTS

10g fresh parsley

30g fresh basil

50g pine nuts

1-2 cloves of garlic

1 tbsp olive oil

75ml stock (chicken or veg)

¼ lemon, juiced

4-6 tbsp room temperature water (optional)

5 tbsp grated Pecorino Romano cheese

Salt and black pepper

METHOD

1. Remove the parsley and basil leaves from the stems, then wash and dry them. Toast the pine nuts until browned all over, then leave to cool completely.

2. Peel and roughly chop the garlic. I always start with 1 clove, then add the second later if I feel the pesto needs it.

3. Now add all the ingredients except the water and grated cheese to a blender, food processor, or pestle and mortar.

4. Blend or crush the ingredients until smooth, gradually adding the water if needed until the pesto reaches your desired consistency. Do this in short bursts if using a blender or processor.

5. Add the grated cheese and give it one last pulse to combine everything, then season to taste with salt and black pepper.

6. Store the pesto in an airtight container or jar in the fridge. If you're going to use this up within about 10 days, then it's fine to keep in the fridge. Any longer than that and I prefer to freeze portions in an ice cube tray to pop out and use as needed.

Tips: Use a low-salt stock or homemade if you can. If you're using a stock pot or cube, make sure to dilute it with the correct amount of water according to the packaging and then just use 75ml of that, otherwise it will be very salty! It's best to use a pestle and mortar for this, so the pesto doesn't heat up which can cause the colour to lose its vibrancy. If using a blender or food processor, avoid this by pulsing the ingredients in short bursts with little breaks between each one.

CALS:	CARBS:	FAT:	PROTEIN:	DIETARY:
43	0.7G	3.9G	1.8G	GF

Cheese Sauce

A cheese sauce is great to have on hand for things like pasta, cauliflower cheese, fish pie, or even as a topping for potatoes. You can customise it easily by adding different flavours, such as pesto or Cajun seasoning, to create loads of variations on this basic version.

INGREDIENTS

300ml skimmed milk

1 tsp wholegrain mustard

1 tsp Dijon mustard

1 tsp garlic granules

1 tsp onion granules

2 tbsp cornflour, mixed with cold water

100g cheddar, finely grated

30g parmesan, finely grated

METHOD

1. Add the milk, mustards, garlic granules, and onion granules to a pan over a gentle heat.

2. Once warmed through, add the cornflour paste and whisk until thickened. Make sure the cornflour has cooked off too; if it still tastes floury, keep mixing!

3. Finally, stir in the cheeses until melted, then season to taste with salt and black pepper.

Tips: The trick with this one is patience; don't add the cheese until you're sure the cornflour is cooked off. By the time you add your cheese, your sauce should already be close to the desired consistency. Add more cornflour mixed to a paste with cold water if it doesn't look as thick as you would like.

CALS:	CARBS:	FAT:	PROTEIN:	DIETARY:
194	10.8G	11.4G	11.7G	GF

Creamy Sundried Tomato Sauce

PREP TIME: 5 MINUTES | COOK TIME: 15 MINUTES | SERVES: 4 (50-75ML SERVINGS)

This sauce is sure to impress as it's simple to make but looks and tastes like restaurant quality! It's amazing on chicken and fish or with rice and pasta dishes.

INGREDIENTS

I white onion, finely diced

4 cloves of garlic, roughly chopped

75g sundried tomatoes, drained and roughly chopped

2 tbsp tomato purée

I tbsp smoked paprika

I tbsp dried oregano

2 tsp dried basil

I tsp black pepper

½ lemon, juiced

300ml stock (chicken or veg)

I tbsp cornflour, mixed with cold water

2 tbsp light cream cheese

30g parmesan, finely grated

150g spinach (optional)

METHOD

1. Spray a pan with oil and fry the onion, garlic and sundried tomatoes until the onion has softened and taken on some colour.

2. Stir in the tomato purée, smoked paprika, oregano, basil, black pepper, and lemon juice, then pour in the stock.

3. Allow this to simmer on a medium heat until reduced and slightly thickened, then stir in the cornflour paste and continue to cook until thickened.

4. Finish the sauce by stirring in the cream cheese, grated parmesan, and spinach if using.

Tips: I often use shallots in this sauce for a subtle sweet flavour, but white or even red onions work too.

CALS:	CARBS:	FAT:	PROTEIN:	DIETARY:
109	8.6G	5.1G	6.2G	GF, VEGGIE (USE A VEGGIE HARD CHEESE)

Roasted Red Pepper Sauce

PREP TIME: 20 MINUTES | COOK TIME: 40 MINUTES | SERVES: 6 (100ML SERVINGS)

This is a great way to hide vegetables for those fussy eaters! It works as a pasta or risotto sauce, but also makes a lovely change from the usual tomato pizza base. It's also great with chicken and pork, and white fish like cod or haddock. I even have it as a snack sometimes, eaten hot like soup.

INGREDIENTS

6 red bell peppers, halved

1 tbsp smoked paprika

2 red onions, roughly chopped

6 cloves of garlic, roughly chopped

3 medium carrots, roughly chopped

400-500ml stock (chicken or veg)

50ml balsamic vinegar

3 tbsp tomato purée

1 tbsp dried oregano

1 tbsp dried basil

2 tsp onion granules

Salt and black pepper

Pinch of sugar

1-2 tbsp light cream cheese/crème fraiche or fat-free Greek yoghurt (optional)

METHOD

1. Spray the halved peppers with oil and then sprinkle with the smoked paprika and some salt. Rub everything in so that the peppers are coated.

2. Roast the peppers in the oven at 180°c for about 30 minutes, then remove and set aside to cool. You can also air fry them at 180°c for 20-25 minutes.

3. Meanwhile, fry the chopped red onions, garlic and carrots in a little cooking oil spray until they have some colour.

4. Cover the veg with the stock, bring to the boil and then simmer on a medium heat until the carrots are fork tender.

5. Once the peppers have roasted, you should easily be able to peel off and discard the skins. Place the peppers in a blender or food processor.

6. Add the vegetables and stock to the blender or food processor and blend until smooth, adding more stock or water to thin out the sauce if necessary.

7. Pour the sauce back into the pan and heat gently. Stir in all the remaining ingredients, seasoning to taste with salt, black pepper, and sugar as needed.

8. To make the sauce extra creamy, you can stir through a tablespoon or two of light cream cheese, light crème fraiche, or fat-free Greek yoghurt before cooling and storing it.

Tips: If you let the roasted peppers rest under some tin foil as soon as they come out of the oven, they will steam a little and then be much easier to peel.

CALS:	CARBS:	FAT:	PROTEIN:	DIETARY:
73	12.4G	0.3G	2.8G	GF, DF, VEGAN

Smoky BBQ Style Sauce

PREP TIME: 5 MINUTES | COOK TIME: 20 MINUTES | SERVES: 4 (75ML SERVINGS)

BBQ sauce is great for marinating or glazing meats, and it makes a delicious pizza base too! It's also great in a cheesy toasted wrap or quesadilla. This BBQ sauce has a lot less sugar than the shop-bought versions, plus some hidden veggies.

INGREDIENTS

1 white onion, roughly chopped

2 red onions, roughly chopped

6 cloves of garlic, chopped

3 tbsp tomato purée

4 tbsp brown sugar

4 tbsp BBQ seasoning

4 tbsp balsamic vinegar

2 tbsp Worcestershire Sauce

2 tbsp smoked paprika

2 tsp oyster sauce

1 tsp chilli powder

1 tsp mustard powder

300ml passata

Salt and black pepper

Sweetener, to taste

METHOD

1. Fry the onions and garlic until beginning to soften, then stir in the tomato purée and brown sugar. Cook until it changes to a deeper shade of red.

2. Stir in the BBQ seasoning, balsamic vinegar, Worcestershire Sauce, smoked paprika, oyster sauce, chilli powder, and mustard powder, then add the passata.

3. Let everything simmer for 15 minutes or so, then season to taste with salt and pepper, and maybe a touch of sweetener if you don't think it's sweet enough at this point.

4. Once the sauce has simmered for at least 15 minutes, you can leave it chunky or blend to a smoother consistency; it's completely up to you!

Tips: Simmer this sauce for a minimum of 15 minutes; if you have time to let it simmer on a really low heat for around 40 minutes, the flavours will develop even more. For an extra smoky flavour, you can add a few drops of 'liquid smoke' which quite a few supermarkets now sell. This always tastes better after being in the fridge overnight!

CALS:	CARBS:	FAT:	PROTEIN:	DIETARY:
192	34G	0.9G	3.2G	DF

Marinara (Tomato) Sauce

This sauce can form the basis of so many meals: pizza and pasta spring to mind of course, but it's also great with chicken – especially chicken parmigiana – and even in wraps and sandwiches too!

INGREDIENTS

1 white onion, finely diced

6 cloves of garlic, finely chopped

75g tomato purée

400g tinned chopped tomatoes

200ml stock (chicken or veg)

50ml balsamic vinegar

1 tbsp dried oregano

1 tbsp dried parsley

1 tbsp dried basil

Salt and black pepper

Pinch of sugar

METHOD

1. Fry the onion and garlic in some cooking oil spray until softened.

2. Stir in the tomato purée and cook until it has turned a deep red colour.

3. Add the chopped tomatoes, stock, balsamic vinegar, and herbs to the pan.

4. Mix well and then simmer the sauce on a medium heat for at least 20 minutes, until reduced and thickened. The longer you let it cook, the more depth of flavour the sauce will have.

5. Season the finished sauce to taste with salt, black pepper and sugar as needed.

Tips: The quality of tinned tomatoes you use will make a huge difference to the flavour of this sauce.

The longer you simmer this for, the richer the flavour will become. If I have time, I simmer mine for over an hour! Just add a splash more stock if it seems like the sauce is becoming too thick or dry.

CALS:	CARBS:	FAT:	PROTEIN:	DIETARY:
71	11.3G	0.4G	3.6G	GF, DF, VEGAN (IF USING VEG STOCK)

Asian Style Peanut Sauce

PREP TIME: 5 MINUTES | SERVES: 8 (50G SERVINGS)

This is an amazing dipping sauce for chicken, prawns, spring rolls, or crunchy veggies like carrots, cucumber and peppers. It's also delicious mixed into noodles or rice, or as a salad dressing!

INGREDIENTS

150g smooth peanut butter
50ml coconut milk drink
4 tbsp light soy sauce
3 tbsp honey
2 limes, juiced
1-2 cloves of garlic, grated
1 tsp grated fresh ginger

OPTIONAL EXTRAS

½ tsp chilli flakes
Chopped peanuts
Fresh coriander

METHOD

1. Mix the peanut butter, coconut milk drink, soy sauce, honey, lime juice, garlic, and ginger together, along with the chilli flakes if using.

2. Stir in some warm water to thin the sauce until it has a consistency you like. For a dipping sauce I like it thicker, but for a salad or noodle dressing, I prefer it a little thinner.

3. You may want to adjust the seasonings to your liking, such as more honey for sweetness or more soy sauce for saltiness.

4. If I am serving this as a dipping sauce, I like to sprinkle crunchy peanuts, chilli flakes and fresh coriander on top to serve!

Tips: Make sure you use coconut milk drink – the one in a carton, found with the milk alternatives – rather than coconut milk in a tin which is usually found on the world foods aisle. You can use crunchy peanut butter instead of smooth; it depends on what consistency you're looking for in this sauce.

CALS:	CARBS:	FAT:	PROTEIN:	DIETARY:
142	7.6G	9.6G	5G	DF, VEGGIE

Asian Style Sticky Sauce

PREP TIME: 5 MINUTES | COOK TIME: 5 MINUTES | SERVES: 4 (50ML SERVINGS)

This sauce is great for whipping up quick and delicious meals; I particularly love it on chicken, salmon or tofu done in the air fryer or pan fried. It also works well on wraps, or with rice or noodles, and it's amazing on crispy battered or breaded chicken too!

INGREDIENTS

90g honey
4 tbsp soy sauce
3 tbsp oyster sauce
2 tbsp sesame oil
½ lime, juiced
2 cloves of garlic, finely chopped
1 tsp grated fresh ginger
Sesame seeds (optional)

METHOD

1. Add all the ingredients to a pan and cook on a high heat until boiling.

2. Turn the heat down to medium and stir continuously for a few minutes, until the sauce has thickened and become sticky.

3. Once the sauce is ready, I like to stir in some sesame seeds if I have them, but this is completely up to you.

Tips: You have to keep an eye on this one; don't leave it alone or stop stirring as it can easily catch on the bottom of the pan!

CALS:	CARBS:	FAT:	PROTEIN:
96	23.1G	0.3G	1.7G

Garlic Yoghurt Sauce

PREP TIME: 5 MINUTES | SERVES: 4 (75ML SERVINGS)

This is probably the sauce I make the most because it's so versatile, and so easy to whip up! I like it on salads, wraps, and kebabs, with all kinds of grilled meat, and on the side with a curry.

INGREDIENTS

300g fat-free Greek yoghurt

1-2 cloves of garlic, finely grated

1 lemon, juiced

2 tsp finely chopped fresh mint

1 tsp finely chopped fresh dill

½ tsp salt

OPTIONAL SEASONINGS

White pepper

Chilli flakes

Sugar

Salt

METHOD

1. Mix all the ingredients together until combined with a smooth texture.

2. Taste the sauce to see if you want to add anything. This might include more garlic, salt, pepper, sugar, or chilli flakes depending on how you like it. I always like lots of garlic! Salt will help if it tastes a bit too acidic for your liking, and chilli flakes add a nice kick if you're someone who enjoys the heat!

3. Stir in cold water, 1 tablespoon at a time, until the sauce reaches your desired consistency. If using as a dip, for example with barbecued meats or a curry, I prefer it thicker whereas if I'm using it as a drizzle on something like kebabs or wraps, I make it slightly thinner.

Tips: You can use dried mint and dill in this if you don't have fresh: just use 1 tsp mint and ½ tsp dill if so.
Always start with just one clove of garlic and taste test after mixing, otherwise you'll have to balance out too much garlic with a lot more yoghurt!

CALS:	CARBS:	FAT:	PROTEIN:	DIETARY:
50	14.6G	0.2G	8.3G	GF, VEGGIE

Balsamic Roasted Green Beans & Tomatoes

PREP TIME: 5 MINUTES | COOK TIME: 15 MINUTES | SERVES: 4

A handful of simple ingredients make up this delicious side dish, which is perfect for meal prep or adding to quick easy dinners.

INGREDIENTS

300g green beans
300g cherry tomatoes
2 tbsp balsamic vinegar
Salt and black pepper

METHOD

1. Top and tail the green beans and halve the cherry tomatoes, then spread them out on a baking tray lined with greaseproof paper.

2. Spray the beans and tomatoes with oil, drizzle over the balsamic vinegar, and season to taste with salt and black pepper.

3. Roast them in the oven for about 15 minutes at 200°c, turning everything halfway through, or cook in the air fryer at 190°c for 8 minutes until you see the green beans begin to brown at the edges.

Tips: For extra flavour, add some grated parmesan to the veg before roasting for a lovely saltiness and a bit of crunch!

CALS:	CARBS:	FAT:	PROTEIN:	DIETARY:
49	6.2G	0.2G	2.4G	GF, DF, VEGAN

Crispy Bacon and Onion Potatoes

PREP TIME: 10 MINUTES | COOK TIME: 15-20 MINUTES | SERVES: 4

These potatoes make a tasty change from the usual chips or mash and can be prepared in advance, then simply heated through in the oven or air fryer (or even microwaved) when you're ready to eat.

INGREDIENTS

500g new potatoes

6 rashers of smoked streaky bacon, chopped

1 white onion, finely chopped

Salt and black pepper

Fresh parsley (optional)

METHOD

1. Parboil the potatoes for approximately 5 minutes, until you can just about push a knife into them. Drain well and set aside to cool.

2. Once they're cool enough to handle, slice the potatoes into pieces about 1-2cm thick. Cover these with a clean tea towel and allow to steam dry.

3. Once they're dry, add the sliced potatoes to a pan with some cooking oil spray in one layer. If you have too many for a single layer, you'll need to use 2 pans or cook them in 2 batches.

4. Once the potatoes begin to get some colour on the bottom, flip them over and add the bacon and onion. Cover with the lid and cook until the bacon is crispy and the onion has softened and browned.

5. You can also cook these in the air fryer. Just add the parboiled potatoes, bacon and onions together, and cook at 180°c for 10-15 minutes until crispy, flipping them halfway through.

6. Season to taste with salt and black pepper, then sprinkle over some fresh parsley to serve.

Tips: Waxy potatoes are better than floury potatoes for this recipe, as the floury potatoes have a tendency to break down and crumble into pieces. Instead of parboiling fresh potatoes, you could use tinned potatoes if you prefer.

CALS:	CARBS:	FAT:	PROTEIN:	DIETARY:
127	16G	3.2G	6.5G	GF, DF

Spinach and Lemon Rice

PREP TIME: 10 MINUTES | COOK TIME: 30 MINUTES | SERVES: 4

This bright and zingy rice is the perfect accompaniment to so many dishes, particularly anything Mediterranean inspired and summery meals such as grilled meats or fish.

INGREDIENTS

1 white onion, finely chopped

4 cloves of garlic, finely chopped

200g fresh spinach

200g long grain rice, washed

475ml stock (chicken or veg)

1 tsp dried dill

1 tbsp finely chopped fresh dill

2 tbsp finely chopped fresh parsley

2 tsp finely chopped fresh chives

1 lemon, zested and juiced

OPTIONAL TOPPINGS

Extra fresh parsley

Lemon wedges

Feta cheese

METHOD

1. Fry the onion on a low-medium heat until softened but not too coloured. Add the garlic and spinach and cook until the garlic is fragrant and the spinach has wilted down.

2. Add the rice, stock and dried dill to the pan. Turn up the heat and bring to the boil, cover with a lid, reduce the heat to low-medium, and simmer for around 20 minutes.

3. Leave the rice to stand with the lid on for 10 minutes off the heat before uncovering and stirring in the fresh herbs, lemon zest and lemon juice before serving.

4. For garnish, I like to add more fresh parsley, lemon wedges, and sometimes feta cheese crumbled over the top too.

Tips: When washing your rice, keep rinsing and draining until the water runs clear.

CALS:	CARBS:	FAT:	PROTEIN:	DIETARY:
235	45G	2.3G	7.5G	**VEGAN** (USE VEGETABLE STOCK)

Smashed Chilli Broccoli

PREP TIME: 15 MINUTES | COOK TIME: 30 MINUTES | SERVES: 4

These smashed broccoli florets work not only as a side dish, but as a delicious snack too: dip them in some sriracha mayo for the perfect spicy bite.

INGREDIENTS

1 head of broccoli
2 tbsp olive oil
2 cloves of garlic, finely chopped
½-1 tsp chilli flakes
Sesame seeds (optional)

METHOD

1. First, place a sieve or metal colander above a pan of simmering water and place the whole broccoli, head side down, into the sieve. Steam for 3-5 minutes until just softened but still bright green in colour. Once cool enough to handle, chop the florets off the head of broccoli.

2. Mix the olive oil with the garlic and chilli flakes, then brush a baking tray with some of the garlic and chilli infused oil.

3. Place the broccoli florets on the baking tray and squash down with the bottom of a jar or a potato masher, then brush the remaining garlic and chilli oil on top of the florets.

4. Bake the broccoli in the oven at 160°c for 20-30 minutes, flipping the florets over after about 15-20 minutes. You can baste them with any remaining oil at this point too.

5. Alternatively, cook the broccoli in the air fryer for about 10 minutes at 160°c. You probably won't need to flip the florets but check on them at the 7-minute mark.

6. I like to sprinkle mine with sesame seeds and some flaky sea salt to serve.

Tips: If you're not a fan of spice, simply skip the chilli flakes and you'll just have delicious garlic smashed broccoli instead!

CALS:	CARBS:	FAT:	PROTEIN:	DIETARY:
63	2.7G	3.9G	3.5G	GF, DF, VEGAN

Charred Sweetcorn Salad

PREP TIME: 10 MINUTES | COOK TIME: 5 MINUTES | SERVES: 4

This crunchy salad goes particularly well with any Mexican style food, but it's a great side dish for most summer recipes and as a snack too!

INGREDIENTS

400g tinned sweetcorn, drained

2 tsp light butter

150g cherry tomatoes, diced

1 orange bell pepper, diced

1 red bell pepper, diced

1 small red onion, diced

5g fresh coriander, roughly chopped

50g feta cheese, crumbled

1 lime, juiced

2 tsp smoked paprika

1 tsp black pepper

1 tsp salt

1 fresh jalapeño, finely chopped (optional)

1 tsp chilli powder (optional)

METHOD

1. Add the sweetcorn to a hot pan with some cooking oil spray and the butter to cook until charred on both sides.

2. Combine the sweetcorn with the tomatoes, bell peppers, onion, coriander, feta cheese, and lime juice.

3. Add the smoked paprika, black pepper and salt as well as the jalapeño and/or chilli powder if using.

4. Mix loosely – you don't want the texture to become mushy – and serve immediately.

Tips: If serving as a snack, you can just eat this by the spoonful – try using tortilla chips as edible cutlery!

CALS:	CARBS:	FAT:	PROTEIN:	DIETARY:
164	18.9G	6.1G	5.7G	GF, VEGGIE

Crispy Cubed Potatoes

PREP TIME: 5 MINUTES | COOK TIME: 30 MINUTES | SERVES: 4

Because they're cubed, these potatoes are extra crunchy and ready in no time. No more soggy chips when you can whip these up instead!

INGREDIENTS

500g potatoes, cut into 2cm cubes

2 tbsp cornflour

1 tbsp smoked paprika

1 tbsp dried oregano

2 tsp dried basil

2 tsp garlic granules

2 tsp onion granules

2 tsp black pepper

2 tsp salt

METHOD

1. Put the cubed potatoes in a bowl with the cornflour and all the seasonings, then spray with oil and toss until they are all evenly coated.

2. Spread the potatoes out on a baking tray in a single layer (use two trays if you don't have enough room) and place in the centre of a preheated oven.

3. Bake at 190°c for 20 minutes, then give them a shake and bake for another 10 minutes at 210°c until they're golden and crispy!

4. You can also make these in the air fryer, which I prefer as they're definitely crispiest this way! They just need 20 minutes at 190°c with a shake around halfway through.

Tips: I don't usually peel the potatoes for this recipe as the skin contains fibre and gets extra crispy when you cook them, plus it saves you a job! However, if you prefer, they will also work when peeled.

CALS:	CARBS:	FAT:	PROTEIN:	DIETARY:
100	21.5G	0.1G	2G	GF, DF, VEGAN

Maple Glazed Sweet Potato Wedges

PREP TIME: 10 MINUTES | COOK TIME: 45 MINUTES | SERVES: 4

Maple syrup and sweet potato are a match made in heaven! These sticky glazed wedges go perfectly with chicken and pork, and really complement any veggie dinners too.

INGREDIENTS

75ml maple syrup

1 tbsp olive oil

1 tsp salt

1 tsp black pepper

500g sweet potatoes, cut into wedges

METHOD

1. Mix the maple syrup, olive oil, salt, and pepper together. Pour this mixture over the sweet potato wedges and toss so that they're fully coated.

2. Remove the wedges from the bowl one by one and place in a single layer on one or more baking trays lined with greaseproof paper. Don't discard any glaze left in the bowl!

3. Bake the wedges in the oven at 180°c for 35 minutes, flipping them after 15 minutes.

4. After 35 minutes, flip the wedges again, brush with any remaining glaze from the bowl, and bake for another 10-15 minutes until soft in the middle, golden and glazed.

Tips: For a touch of saltiness that elevates these wedges even further, I sometimes serve them with crispy bacon pieces sprinkled on top!

CALS:	CARBS:	FAT:	PROTEIN:	DIETARY:
191	34.5G	3.7G	3.25G	GF, DF, VEGAN

Parmesan Roasted Parsnips

PREP TIME: 10 MINUTES | COOK TIME: 30 MINUTES | SERVES: 4

These crunchy, golden parsnips go really well with any dish that has a sauce (they are delicious dipped into anything) and make a great alternative to chips if you fancy something a bit different!

INGREDIENTS

500g parsnips, cut into equal batons

60g parmesan, finely grated

3 tbsp plain flour

1 tbsp dried thyme

2 tsp black pepper

METHOD

1. Parboil the parsnips in a pan of salted boiling water for around 3-5 minutes until they just begin to soften around the edges.

2. Drain and leave in a sieve or colander over the pan with a clean tea towel over the top to absorb the steam. Meanwhile, mix the parmesan, flour, thyme, and black pepper together.

3. Once the parsnips are dry and cool, spray with oil and add them to the parmesan mixture. Toss everything together and make sure the parsnips are fully coated.

4. Spread them out in a single layer on a baking tray lined with greaseproof paper and sprayed with a little oil.

5. Bake the parsnips in the oven at 180°c for about 25 minutes, or in the air fryer for 20-25 minutes at the same temperature, until golden and crispy. You can give them a shake halfway through to help them cook evenly.

Tips: If you want to make these veggie, simply use a vegetarian hard cheese instead of parmesan.

You can swap the thyme for another herb to match your meal; for example, I like to use oregano if I'm having something Italian with these parsnips.

CALS:	CARBS:	FAT:	PROTEIN:	
189	22.1G	6G	8.3G	

Roasted Garlic & Chive Mash

PREP TIME: 10 MINUTES | COOK TIME: 1 HOUR 10 MINUTES | SERVES: 8

I love this hearty side dish on a cold evening! The roasted garlic is so delicious and sweet, and it really elevates a meal. It's great for prepping in advance too, perfect for celebrations or dinner parties.

INGREDIENTS

1 small bulb of garlic

1 tsp olive oil

1kg floury potatoes (Maris Piper or King Edwards work well), cut into 3cm cubes

2 stock cubes (chicken or veg)

10g fresh chives, finely chopped

75ml skimmed milk

1 tbsp light butter

METHOD

1. Chop the top off your garlic bulb, and place it cut side up in some tin foil. Drizzle with the olive oil and sprinkle over some salt (sea salt or flaky salt is best if you have it!).

2. Wrap the garlic in tin foil and place on a tray, then bake in the oven for 50-60 minutes at 180°c until golden brown and soft.

3. Once the garlic is cool enough to handle, squeeze out the softened cloves and mash them using the back of a knife or fork.

4. While the garlic is roasting, make the mash. Cover the cubed potatoes with water in a large pan and add the stock cubes, then boil until the potatoes are fork tender.

5. Drain the potatoes, keeping around 200ml of the starchy stock they were cooked in, then let them steam dry in a colander or sieve on top of the pan with a clean tea towel over the top.

6. Once the potatoes have drained and steam dried, discard any liquid in the bottom of the pan and tip them back in to mash. Use a potato ricer if you have one for the fluffiest mash!

7. Add the roasted garlic, chives, milk and butter to the potatoes and continue to mash until it begins to look creamy. If you want your mash to be even smoother, add some of the reserved stock and mix in with a spatula.

8. Season the mash to taste with salt and pepper (it may not need salt if you added stock).

Tips: This makes a big batch of mashed potatoes, so I like to use half straightaway and freeze the other half to use for an easy meal in the future.

CALS:	CARBS:	FAT:	PROTEIN:	DIETARY:	
142	27G	1.3G	3.8G	GF (CHECK THE STOCK CUBE), VEGGIE	

Acknowledgements

Thank you to all my amazing family and friends who helped with this book – the taste testers, 'sous chefs', and everyone who encouraged and supported me throughout the whole process (and many meltdowns!). For my parents, Grandma and siblings, your words of encouragement and belief in me always helped me to pull through in my wavering moments of self-doubt and I couldn't have done it without you – thank you so much.

I wanted to give a huge special thanks to everyone who helped out on the long shoot days: Mum, Dad, Grandma, Carys, Nicola, Tammy, Gabs, Emma, and Cara. I feel so lucky and grateful to have such supportive and generous people in my life, and I cannot thank you all enough!

Thanks so much to the whole team at Meze Publishing, who made this book possible and turned a dream into a reality! Thank you for working tirelessly to get everything together so quickly and create something I'm so proud of. And thank you for dealing with my constant tweaks to make everything perfect. I appreciate all your help and expertise more than you know!

This book wouldn't have come together so beautifully without the photographs from Timm Cleasby – thank you for executing my vision perfectly. It is always a pleasure to work with you and your photographs are truly amazing!

Thank you to everyone who follows me on social media, for believing in this book and supporting Bec's Bites up to this point. What started as me literally sharing what I was having for tea each night has turned into a huge community, and now a real-life recipe book… I can't quite believe it myself! I really wanted this to be a book that was practical, healthy and delicious – I had such an amazing time creating (and testing!) all the recipes, and I can only hope you enjoy making and eating them as much as I did! Please let me know on social media if you make any – find me @becs.bites on Instagram, TikTok and Facebook.